FAITH WITH REASON

Faith with Reason

PAUL HELM

CLARENDON PRESS · OXFORD

OXFORD

UNIVERSITY PRESS

Great Clarendon Street, Oxford OX2 6DP

Oxford University Press is a department of the University of Oxford.
It furthers the University's objective of excellence in research, scholarship,
and education by publishing worldwide in

Oxford New York

Athens Auckland Bangkok Bogotá Buenos Aires Calcutta
Cape Town Chennai Dar es Salaam Delhi Florence Hong Kong Istanbul
Karachi Kuala Lumpur Madrid Melbourne Mexico City Mumbai
Nairobi Paris São Paulo Singapore Taipei Tokyo Toronto Warsaw
and associated companies in Berlin Ibadan

Oxford is a registered trade mark of Oxford University Press
in the UK and in certain other countries

Published in the United States
by Oxford University Press Inc., New York

© Paul Helm 2000

The moral rights of the author have been asserted
Database right Oxford University Press (maker)

First published 2000

British Library Cataloguing in Publication Data
Data available

Library of Congress Cataloging in Publication Data
Data available

ISBN 0-19-823845-2

1 3 5 7 9 10 8 6 4 2

Typeset by Hope Services (Abingdon) Ltd.
Printed in Great Britain
on acid-free paper by
Biddles Ltd
Guildford and King's Lynn

For Alice

PREFACE

All except one of the chapters of this book was first delivered as the 1996 Stanton Lectures in the School of Divinity, University of Cambridge. I wish to thank the Electors to the Lectureship for inviting me to deliver them and Professor Nicholas Lash and his colleagues for their friendship and hospitality over the weeks during which the lectures were given. Chapter 4 started life as an 'emergency' presidential lecture given at the 1997 Conference of the British Society for the Philosophy of Religion, Oriel College, Oxford. An earlier version of part of Chapter 8 appears in *Faith and Reason*, ed. Paul Helm (Oxford, 1999), 375–8.

The task of transforming lectures into chapters, which proved more difficult than at first I imagined it was going to be, has been greatly helped by the readers to whom the original manuscript was sent. I am grateful to them for their painstaking criticism and advice, as I am to Peter Momtchiloff of the Press for his patience and encouragement, and especially to my wife Angela for her continual support.

P. H.
King's College, London

CONTENTS

Introduction   xiii

1. Can Faith be Discussed?   I

   Five Reasons for Not Discussing Faith   3
   Concepts of Faith   15
   Conclusion   20

2. Faith and Foundationalism   21

   Strong Foundationalism and its Weaknesses   22
   Kenny's Response   27
   Foundationalism and Beyond   38

3. The Web of Belief   43

   Strategic Order   43
   The Web   49
   Coherence   53
   Objections   58
   The Web of Belief and the Nature of Faith   62

4. Accumulated Evidence   66

   Resolving Disputes by Rational Means   68
   The Person-relativity of Religious Belief   72
   The Nature of Religion   78
   Conclusion   82

5. Belief and Believing   84

   Accounting for Unbelief   87
   The Fact of Bias   89
   Facts and Values: Their Connectedness   93
   Objections   98

6. 'The Believer'   102

   'Thin' and 'Thick' Belief and Believing   103

x *Contents*

The Instability of Thick Believing   111

7. What Is It to Trust God?   119

   Conceptual Preconditions   122
   Interests   125
   Interpersonal Relations   129
   God and Evidence   132
   Bare Particularity   136
   Conclusion   137

8. Faith and Virtue   139

   Faith and Belief   141
   A Paradox?   144
   Trust   149
   The Evidential Proportion View of Faith   153

9. Faith and Self-reflection   158

   Faith and Assurance   159
   The Conditions of Assurance   162
   Faith and Self-reflection   165
   Faith and Conditionality   170
   The Faith and Conditions Argument   171
   The Grounds Substitution Argument   175

Bibliography   179

Index   183

Just as right order requires that we believe the deep matters of the Christian faith before we discuss them rationally, so it seems to me to be an instance of carelessness if, having been confirmed in faith, we do not eagerly desire to understand what we believe.

Anselm, *Cur Deus Homo*

INTRODUCTION

This book is mainly concerned with some issues to do with reasonable religious belief. Religious belief has to meet and sustain philosophical scrutiny as does any other belief; nothing about religion purchases immunity from this. This is the claim of the first chapter. But at the same time religious epistemology has also to respect the contours of religion, just as, say, moral epistemology has to respect the contours of morality. It has to recognize that if some religious beliefs are reasonable they may well be so in virtue of respecting the distinctive subject-matter of the belief, and refusing to allow that it is reducible to some other subject-matter. What I refer to as the James Principle, the claim of William James that 'A rule of thinking which would absolutely prevent me from acknowledging certain kinds of truth, if those kinds of truth were really there, would be an irrational rule', has to be carefully observed.

An important feature of philosophy is that it proceeds step by step, argument by argument. As religious belief has been held under a very wide variety of intellectual circumstances and conditions, there is no alternative but to look at these arguments one at a time, for at any one time there are likely to be myriads of ways of defending the rationality of religious belief, depending upon what counts as a defence, what rationality is taken to be, and what a particular religious belief amounts to. The idea of religious faith is, in particular, a rich and confusing field, and the first chapter closes by drawing attention to various distinctive kinds of religious faith, and in particular to the belief component of such faith; in particular to what I call the *evidential proportion* and the *evidential deficiency* views of faith. Under such circumstances in philosophizing about religion there is no escape from a case by case, line by line approach.

From this enormous field of possible ways of exploring the rationality of religious belief the second, third, and fourth chapters single out two currently prominent epistemological strategies. The first of these, associated with 'Reformed' epistemology, argues that it is reasonable to believe that God exists (and also to believe much more about God) without argument. Chapter 2 offers a partial defence of this position against some criticisms levelled against it by Anthony Kenny.

Although some form of foundationalism is defensible, the linear reasoning that is often associated with it (though not entailed by it) does not do justice to the idea of narrative which is central to making the Christian religion intelligible and defensible. And so the second reasonableness strategy that I examine and defend is a cumulative case for theism, a case in which the intelligibility of a narrative plays an important role. A cumulative case is a set of arguments which reinforce each other, as different lines of evidence might reinforce the conviction that a particular person committed a crime. So Chapter 3 defends a coherentist account of epistemic justification of religious faith in which there is no principled distinction between non-inferential and inferential beliefs.

Chapter 4 explores aspects of Basil Mitchell's accumulation strategy and highlights, besides straightforward beliefs about matters of fact, two other types of belief that are relevant to faith. The first of these is person-relative beliefs, beliefs which as a matter of fact not everyone has, and which perhaps not everyone can now have. And the second is beliefs about oneself, about one's own wants, fears, and aspirations. The presence and influence of such states is crucial for motivating trust.

So the reasonableness of faith depends not only on beliefs about the world, general beliefs and beliefs which only one person, or a group of people, may in fact hold, but also on beliefs about oneself. For the action of trusting involves not only the believer's estimation of what is true but also of what is of value or importance to him, and also the willingness to rely upon what he takes to be true and valuable.

Chapter 4 concludes by exploring some of the consequences of the fact that these two sorts of beliefs may be at odds with each other. A person may want what God cannot give, and so cease to believe that this God exists (though so desperate may he be to believe in something that he may believe in an idol). Alternatively a person may want what God, if he exists, can give, but lack evidence, or sufficient evidence, for God's existence, and so despair. The requirements for the rationality of religious adherence may be different from those of religious belief.

Bearing in mind the James Principle, what is noteworthy about the object of Christian religious belief is that God has a moral character that is essential to his nature; belief in God is thus not like believing in a morally neutral or morally indifferent matter of fact. Chapter 5 offers tentative support for the idea that one reason for failure to believe may be that the one who fails to believe has an interest in not believing. This chapter explores the connection between having an interest and the appreciation of evidence. There are three questions here: Are at least some failures to believe like the failure to recognize an obligation, like having a moral block? Are other failures like situations where one recognizes an obligation but, due to weakness of will, fails to honour it? And is it always rational, in the interests of objectivity, to suppress the influence of our moral nature as far as possible in our assessment of evidence?

In Chapter 6 we turn our attention away from the wholly evidential or epistemic aspects of religious faith to its fiducial component. Faith is not simply belief, it is also trust. I distinguish between two kinds of belief: a merely theoretical belief, 'thin' belief, and 'thick' belief, belief which has fiducial aspects to it; it is cognitive belief which does not rely upon an account of knowledge and belief which is wholly theoretical in character. Economy of time and effort, as well as the personal interests of the believer, enter into thick belief in a way in which it is totally absent from the theoretical attitude. Belief in the 'thick' sense is required to do justice to the practical demands of faith, and especially to its connection with matters that are valued by the one who believes. Such a belief is capable of rational defence, and it may be defended rationally by considerations which are, as far as the evidential side of things is concerned, different and less stringent than in the case of thin belief. The chapter attempts to explore the interconnection between the two senses of belief, in particular the instability of thick belief, its tendency to split apart into either an attitude of thin belief, or a purely aspirational account of faith.

But perhaps despite all that has been said so far it could be argued that religious faith is *sui generis*, that trusting God is a different kind of activity from trusting a suspension bridge, that the word is used purely equivocally in the two cases. In Chapter 7 I examine arguments in favour of such a claim but do not find them convincing.

In Chapter 8 I apply the account of belief and faith that I have been developing in earlier chapters, the evidential proportion view, as I have put it, according to which the strength of trust in an object of trust ought to be proportioned to the strength of belief, to the problem of the relation between faith and action, or faith and virtue. I do not consider the question of whether faith is itself a virtue, but rather take up some of the connections and dislocations between faith and the moral virtues. One contemporary philosopher who has paid considerable attention to the relation between faith and virtue is Professor Richard Swinburne. We focus on the question which runs like a central theme through his treatment of faith, 'May a scoundrel be a man of faith?' The chapter concludes by making a further comparison between the view of faith favoured by Professor Swinburne and the evidential proportion view.

Faith, then, including religious faith, is not simply faith for which there is good evidence for what is trusted in, but also includes a set of beliefs about what is desirable. So at least some kinds of religious faith involve two sorts of beliefs: beliefs about oneself, and beliefs about things other than oneself. In the final chapter we consider one such belief about oneself, namely the belief that I am myself a believer. I explore the logic of the relation between religious belief and the assurance of faith and conclude with a discussion of certain current theological misapprehensions about the conditionality of religious faith, misapprehensions that arise from a mistake about the status of beliefs about oneself.

I

Can Faith be Discussed?

You might well expect that the question, Can faith be discussed?, admits of the answer 'Yes'. Otherwise we could very quickly bring this discussion to a close. And you would be correct to expect this. Faith *can* be discussed. To be more precise, faith can be discussed philosophically. Surprisingly, perhaps, the question of whether faith can be discussed is sometimes raised in the vein of a philosophical question, and sometimes answered negatively on philosophical grounds. It is with these negative philosophical arguments that we shall largely be concerned in this chapter.

I begin by making what you may think is a pedantic point, to stress that as far as I am concerned the philosophy of religion has to do with the philosophical issues that a concrete, historical religion raises or has raised. The philosophy of religion is not a particular type of philosophy, as the wines of the Loire are a particular type of wine, and the fact that some aspect or other of a religion is being addressed does not give us licence to depart from usual standards of philosophical strictness and rigour. Rather, to vary the illustration, philosophy is to religion as civil engineering is to bridge-building; just as a civil engineer may turn his attention away from the construction of bridges to the building of dams, say, so the philosopher may disengage from religion and re-engage with, say, logic or morality. No doubt when, for example, the nature of God is being addressed philosophically, human thought is put under great strain, but that is a different matter, and one that will not largely concern us.

The philosophy of religion is not to be confused, either, with the religion of philosophy; no doubt for some people philosophy does duty for religion, and no doubt philosophy has religious roots. But I shall take philosophy to be a free-standing discipline of long pedigree in Western culture which has to do with the rigorous and clear examination of the meaning and truth of almost any general issue of human interest, including the issues of religion. But philosophy, understood in this way, is not static; as philosophy itself changes and develops, as new issues of human interest are confronted and new arguments developed, so issues in religion may be cast in a new light, seen from a new angle.

Part of the reason for mistakenly thinking that the philosophy of religion is a subject in its own right, and not the application of philosophy to the problems of religion, is that it has become customary to think of *religion* as distinct from religions, plural. No doubt there are philosophical problems common to all religions; but much of the philosophical interest in religion lies in the theological and religious positions within an actual religion, with its own developed theology, both natural and revealed, and with its theological traditions. There are good substantive and methodological reasons for concentrating upon the concrete, whether on particular expressions of Christianity or of another religion; little to be gained, by contrast, by a sort of lowest common denominator approach. This is particularly so in Christianity, where interactions between it and philosophy have been so rich. The interactions between philosophy and 'religion' are, by contrast, feeble and impoverished, and likely to remain so. Hence in what is to follow I shall make no further apology for concentrating, from time to time, on the particularities of Christianity.

But there is another reason for focusing on philosophical aspects of a particular religion. If the religion which we philosophize about is wholly the result of our needs, whether speculative or practical, and not the product of reason and revelation, then our philosophizing about it will be trivial. As George Schlesinger has recently put it,

I believe the theist should refrain from making up the rules of religion as he goes; otherwise, his entire endeavour may become as pointless as 'playing tennis without a net'. It may prove harmful as well, because of its tendency to encourage undisciplined thought, generating anchorless and therefore fickle faith.[1]

What is distinctive of the philosophy of religion, as opposed to other branches of philosophy, if anything is, is that many of its problems arise in the juxtaposition of issues which in other areas of philosophy are treated separately. Thus there is a long philosophical tradition of discussion of free will, and equally long traditions of discussion of the nature of time, and of knowledge; it is only in the problem of the compatibility or otherwise of divine foreknowledge and human free-

[1] George Schlesinger, *New Perspectives on Old-time Religion* (Oxford, 1988), 69–70.

dom, a problem that arises in Judaeo-Christian theism and in Islam, that discussion of these three issues comes together in a unique way. Anyone who is going to make a contribution to this debate will need to have some theological awareness, but more importantly will need to be well versed in the philosophy of all three areas. And when we shall shortly begin to look at some of the issues of faith and reason we shall need to be versed not only in epistemology, but also in ethics and in action theory.

However, despite all that, not everyone would agree. The logical space which ought to be occupied by philosophical discussion of religion is often constricted and misshaped by those who speak about religion in the name of philosophy. Certain current doctrines and attitudes amongst theologians and philosophers of religion seem to me to inhibit full philosophical discussion of religious issues, and I should like to say something about these, and to try to persuade you that they are mistaken and that there is nothing about the Christian religion, or any other mainstream religion, which inhibits a full philosophical discussion of its claims. In doing so I am trying to keep clear some of the space for philosophy to properly consider issues raised in religion. John Locke's conception of the philosopher was as an underlabourer. But sometimes the thickets are so dense that the ground first needs to be cleared before the underlabourer can get to work.

FIVE REASONS FOR NOT DISCUSSING FAITH

The *first* of the current doctrines that I shall discuss which inhibits philosophical investigation of faith is the claim that religious faith is personal, not propositional, in character. It is frequently said, by theologians of a philosophical turn, but also by some philosophers of religion, that the central religious stance, faith in God, cannot be propositional in form, but must be personal. Indeed, in a recent survey of different ideas of faith, such a view gets considerable discussion.[2] What such a personalist view of faith means, I think, is that the concept of religious faith cannot be understood in terms of anything that is or contains a propositional component, a that-clause followed

---

[2] William Lad Sessions, *The Concept of Faith* (Ithaca, NY, 1994).

by an expression capable of having a truth-value. Faith does not involve belief. Faith is 'faith in', not 'faith that'; faith in God cannot be understood in terms of a set of beliefs that. On such a view faith is non-propositional, and therefore non-doxastic, in character. I am aware that some philosophers, for example Robert Audi,[3] argue that it is possible to identify a case of non-doxastic and yet propositional faith, though I find this implausible. In contrast to this idea I shall take it that faith is essentially doxastic and therefore propositional while recognizing that it has non-doxastic aspects, and that there are circumstances where its usage is primarily attitudinal (where, for example, certain beliefs are taken for granted). But it can only be attitudinal because it is propositional, and, I shall assume, doxastic.

But faith, though doxastic, does not reduce to a set of propositional beliefs; belief is not sufficient for faith, for besides such beliefs there is a fiduciary element, trust. And this in turn involves two things: that there is something or someone to trust (and this involves beliefs about the trustworthiness of the object of faith, at least if a measure of referential transparency is assumed), and that what is worth trusting is actually trusted.

But in saying that faith is personal the proponents of such an idea characteristically mean more than that it is wholly attitudinal and not doxastic in character. In saying that faith is personal, it is implied that any attempt to understand what faith is from a non-participatory standpoint, a standpoint 'outside' that of the believer, subverts faith, or causes it to disintegrate. Faith only retains its integrity as faith so long as it is unselfconscious and engaged in a relationship with its object in such a way that the object absorbs the entire attention of the believer. If this were true, it would inhibit philosophical discussion of religion in a systematic way, in rather the way in which a deeply personal relationship would change in character if the relationship were being continually analysed. Such a view would mean that any reflective account of any kind (including a philosophical account) of the personal relation that is at the heart of religion must be a falsification of that relationship, since, it is claimed, any such account is an attempt to set out in an objective way, a way that is comprehensible to participants and non-participants alike, what is a

---

[3] Robert Audi, 'Faith, Belief and Rationality', in James E. Tomberlin (ed.), *Philosophical Perspectives 5: Philosophy of Religion, 1991* (Atascadero, Calif., 1991).

relation between subjects and so is incapable of being given objective expression.

One may freely allow that propositional expressions, as these occur in our various propositional attitudes, are selective. They pick out for attention, from the seamless web of our experience of the world, some feature of that experience, or some hypothetical or counterfactual situation. In so doing they abstract from the phenomenological feltness of the experience, its immediacy and richness, which they partly describe. But this is so whether that experience is, say, the detached observing of some object in the world, or a personal relation of mutual trust. Both observing and relating are part of the seamless web of experience, and are aspects of that web which may be identified for discussion. The proposition, if it is a true proposition, represents some aspect of this complex experience in propositional form. But why does such representation invariably lead to mischaracterization or to distortion, provided that we are aware of the fact of selectivity? And surely trust may survive reflection, and even be enhanced by it, even though inordinate reflection would subvert it.

The argument that faith cannot be doxastic and therefore propositional in character because propositions are detached, theoretical, static, and timeless, but faith involves dynamic commitment, can be quickly dismissed. It all depends upon the proposition. Some propositions[4] are theoretical and timeless; they are true for all time, or true in a way that is indifferent to time, and they may also be of only theoretical interest. 'Hyperion is among Saturn's fifteen moons', for example. But others are practical and timely, of intense and immediate interest. The point would quickly be demonstrated if someone convincingly said that a bomb is about to go off in here, or that the person with the bleeding hand has AIDS.

It is true that we often use the expression 'faith in', just as we use 'belief in' (either as a synonym for 'faith in' or as short for 'belief in the existence or worth of'). But it should be clear that such faith (or belief, where it is synonymous with trust) is always exercised in respect of some belief or beliefs about the one in whom the faith is exercised. Normally to assert that one has faith in the narrow bridge suspended across the ravine, if it does not *mean*, certainly *entails*, that it is in virtue of some facts about or features of the bridge, facts or

---

[4] There is a more technical sense of 'proposition' in which propositions are necessarily timeless, but I am not employing that sense here.

features that are expressible in terms of my believing that such and such is true of the bridge, that I have faith in the bridge. And even if, in an utterly idiosyncratic way, in the spirit of Kierkegaard, one were to detach faith from any positive grounds or reasons at all, and to say that one had faith in God simply *because* there were and could be no grounds or reasons to have such faith, the that-clause would not thereby be eliminated. Faith would entail belief, even if the belief were groundless.

Of course to say that faith is propositional, or necessarily involves propositions, is not to say that the faith is *in* the proposition and not in the reality which the proposition denotes and describes, as some perversely seem to think. The proposition believed does not interpose itself between ourselves and reality, obscuring reality in the way that a distorting mirror or tinnitus may; rather it expresses some aspect of that reality. Typically, it identifies that aspect by picking out some subject by means of a referring expression, a name or pronoun or a definite description, and then by saying something about what has thus been picked out. What it is able to say about what is picked out is limited by the semantics at its disposal. For this and for other reasons any proposition, however complex, can pick out only *some* aspect of the reality to which it refers. But it should go without saying that the reality is not and cannot be a set of propositions; the bridge, say, is a real physical object and not a set of abstract propositions. God is a real object of attention, whereas propositions about him are intentional objects; if there were no creaturely thoughts about God his reality would not be impaired. But beliefs about God or the bridge are expressed in propositions; though, again, never exhaustively, since any physical object, and most other objects of attention, may give rise to an inexhaustible supply of truths about themselves and the other things to which they are or may be related.

What is offered in place of the view that faith is propositional? It is said that faith is personal. Well, if by this is meant that faith can be faith in a person, and the faith of a person, the point can be granted. But not if 'personal' and 'propositional' are opposed in this way: personal and *therefore* not propositional. This opposition seems facile; why should we accept it? If I trust you I trust you in virtue of something about you, something real or imaginary, which can be expressed in propositional form.

It may be said that my objections to the personal view of faith simply beg the question in favour of a view of faith that involves belief.

But this is not at all clear. Even if we suppose a view of faith which takes the object of faith to be a matter of direct acquaintance, perhaps even a case of knowledge by acquaintance, the same point holds. I trust you in virtue of certain facts or possible facts about you made apparent in my awareness; because I see your clear blue eyes and gimlet chin, facts about you expressible only in propositions or perhaps, more cumbersomely, as states of affairs; for example, I trust you because of your clear blue eyes. It is hardly relevant that I may not have time to articulate the features which make you trustworthy before I actually trust you.

A *second* claim made by philosophers of religion which inhibits the philosophical discussion of faith is that belief in God is not a belief in a matter of fact. This is said by, among others, D. Z. Phillips[5] and is regarded by him as a point of some importance. It goes along with saying that the issue of the existence of God is not an 'external' fact. Such philosophers may be asserting a number of things here. It is true that the question of the existence of God is not an isolated issue. Much, cognitively speaking, may hang on it, and so if the existence of God is denied, then much else will be or may be denied. For example, if God does not exist, then the question of whether the universe is created is settled—it isn't; as is the question of whether there will be an afterlife in his presence—there won't be; and so on. And other questions may be settled: whether there are objective moral facts, for example; perhaps even whether it is rational to trust one's senses. But there are hosts of mundane facts which are related in such ways as these. To say of a proposition that it expresses a matter of fact cannot be to say that it is contingently related to all other facts. It is a fact about me that I am not now in Australia; from this follows a vast number of other facts—that I am not in Sydney, that I am not in Brisbane, and so on. But this phenomenon, the interconnectedness of sets of contingent facts, does not mean that the belief that I am not at present in Australia is not a matter of fact.

It is certainly true that if God exists he is in some sense a necessary being. So the existence of God is not a mere matter of fact in at least one sense of that term; his existence is not causally dependent on the existence of other beings or powers, but they exist because of him. And if Anselm and the perfect being theologians are correct, not only does God not exist contingently, because he is

---

[5] D. Z. Phillips, *Faith and Philosophical Enquiry* (London, 1970), 3.

causally necessary and has his existence *a se*, his existence is also logically necessary.

I shall not go into the question of whether causally necessary existence makes sense, but assume that it does. Belief in God, in that case, is certainly belief in the existence of someone both strange and wonderful, a necessary being. But does this make belief in the existence of God any less a matter of fact?

Something else that may be meant by this claim, the claim that belief in the existence of God is not belief in a matter of fact, is that such belief cannot be held in a casual or in an indifferent way. Anyone who truly understands what the existence of God means cannot be indifferent to it. Furthermore, God's existence is, for Phillips, the foundation of a whole form of life, and therefore necessary to it. Even if these things are so, this does not rule out belief in God from being a matter of fact. I shall have more to say in a subsequent chapter about whether such casual belief is possible, whether it makes sense to say 'I believe that God exists but I could not care less.'

A *third* inhibitor of true philosophical discussion of faith is the thesis that in religion understanding and believing are inseparable. It is generally and uncontroversially held that understanding a proposition, some understanding of it, is a necessary condition of believing it. (One might have implicit faith, though this is a case that raises other issues.) At the very least, if I believe that *p*, then I must have some understanding of the meaning of some sentence which expresses *p*. And perhaps I need also to understand some of the grounds for thinking that *p* is true. It is widely held, in the faith-seeks-understanding tradition in Christian thought, that understanding and believing are connected in that faith is also a condition of further understanding.[6] A person believes in order to gain more understanding. But in saying that understanding and believing are inseparable, more than this is being claimed: not merely that some understanding is *necessary* for belief, but that it is *sufficient* for belief. One cannot understand without believing.

What this means appears to be something like the following: to understand is to believe, and as understanding may be a matter of degree, so may believing be. It is only as one understands that one comes to have faith; in understanding, in gaining appreciation of, the

[6] See Paul Helm, *Faith and Understanding* (Edinburgh, 1997).

language game of religion, with its characteristic values and significances, one gains faith. Not to understand is not to believe. On the face of things, this seems a curious claim. There are surely many sentences which as soon as they are understood, they are definitely not believed. As soon as you hear me sincerely utter the sentence 'We are all in Brisbane' you definitely do not believe it. There are other propositions which as soon as they are understood are believed to a degree, for example the proposition 'Most people here have eaten fish in the last week'; and there are other propositions which, on being understood, elicit firm and undeviating belief, for example 'I am now reading this page.' The relationship between understanding and believing seems to be a wholly variable one. The credibility of a belief depends upon evidence, on grounds, and the relation between the existence of such evidence and understanding the proposition in question is always a contingent one.

The propositions of religion and theology seem to be no exception to this. As Anthony Kenny has remarked,

Many theological doctrines, whether or not they are true, seem perfectly intelligible to the unbeliever: for instance, the doctrine of the resurrection. It may take faith to believe that Jesus rose on the third day; but there is no difficulty in understanding what is meant by the doctrine.[7]

Furthermore, where one *identifies* understanding and believing, as Phillips and others do, obvious problems arise; in particular, the problem of how one may then give an intelligible and persuasive account of the rejection by some of the same proposition believed by others. Or, to put the matter more dramatically, how can one give an account of religious rebellion? For surely the point about rebellion, what makes it a case of such, is that a person knowingly rejects the very same matter that others accept, and that he might have accepted. But if disbelieving and believing a claim involve a common understanding of it, then believing and understanding cannot be the same thing. For if believing and understanding go hand in hand, then rejection, which involves unbelief, or at least non-belief, must always, as a matter of definition, involve misunderstanding, even if it is not the result of misunderstanding. So on this view no one ever rejects Christianity, one only ever rejects misunderstandings of it;[8]

---

[7] Anthony Kenny, *What is Faith?* (Oxford, 1992), 66–7.

[8] A similar point, this time about the relation between reason and revelation in a more explicitly theological context, is well made by Kathryn Tanner in 'Jesus Christ',

because if such a person truly understood Christianity they would believe its characteristic doctrines, since understanding is believing. This may be a convenient and even a comforting doctrine, at least for the practitioners of Christianity (or of any other religion), but it seems obviously false.

The point can be made more economically and austerely using an argument of Frege's. In the valid argument, 'p is revealed by God; if p is revealed by God then p is true; therefore p is true', 'p' occurs first asserted and then (as the antecedent of a conditional proposition) as unasserted. So assertion cannot be a part of meaning. Otherwise the argument just given would not be valid. And so 'p' must have the same meaning whether p is revealed by God or not.[9]

Phillips offers two answers to this type of objection. The first is to allow that there is a place for rejection in religion provided one understands this as the rejection of an entire 'form of life'. The one who rejects or rebels in effect says 'Religion means nothing to me.' That is, the rebel dismisses the whole religious way of thinking about the world and of engaging with it. That there are such cases may be granted, but there is a shift in the meaning of 'meaning' here. Someone who says 'Religion means nothing to me' is not saying that the characteristic propositions of religion are meaningless; rather, he is saying that the idea of a religious way of life has no personal significance for him. This is a rather different point, but one that can intelligibly be made only on the assumption that there is some understanding of what religion is, and what the claims of a religion mean, on the part of the one who rejects that way of life. Otherwise, what is he rejecting? It may be precisely *because* he understands what a particular religion implies that a person may want nothing to do with it.

But what about rejection not as the rejection of an entire language game, but like the rejection of the prophet Jonah, who fled from before the presence of the Lord? The case of someone who has some understanding of the concept of God, believes that he exists, and believes many other things about him, but wants nothing to do with him? In answer to this Phillips says that 'belief in God' has a wider application than 'belief in John', in that a person whose basic relation to God was one of fear may none the less believe in God. Phillips endorses the following claim made by Norman Malcolm:

her contribution to *The Cambridge Companion to Christian Doctrine*, ed. Colin E. Gunton (Cambridge, 1997), 264 ff.

    [9] Cf. P. T. Geach, 'Assertion', in *Logic Matters* (Oxford, 1972), 254 f.

Belief in God encompasses not only trust but also awe, dread, dismay, resentment, and perhaps even hatred. Belief in God will involve some affective state or attitude, having God as its object, and those attitudes could vary from reverential love to rebellious rejection.[10]

So in the face of the objection about rebellion there is *some* modification of Phillips's thesis; he modifies the sense of 'belief' that is relevant. But this, once again, looks to be a stipulative response to the problem. Phillips simply defines belief in God in a way that suits exactly what he wishes to say about religion as a language game. Understanding and believing go hand in hand, but believing includes not only trust but fear. Apart from noting the stipulation, there are two replies that may be made to such a claim.

We need to distinguish between belief in (the existence of) God, and belief (trust) in God. Hatred of God involves belief in the existence of God, but it does not involve trust in him. So why should hatred of God be regarded as an instance of belief in God? Phillips appears to trade on the ambiguity of 'belief in God' as between 'belief in the existence of' and 'trust'. Someone who is said to believe in God but who hates God in the sense meant by Malcolm and Phillips can hardly be said to trust him, but rather to believe that it is true that God exists, and for that reason to fear him.

Even on Phillips's own admission there is one proposition, 'God exists', which may arouse trust in *A* and hatred in *B*. But why should authentic responses be restricted to trust and fear? Why may not one response be indifference, indifference to the question of whether God exists? Why must all the intelligible religious attitudes be *strong* attitudes? (Here, surely, is another case where description and prescription are blurred together.) Why may not someone believe that God exists and be indifferent to the fact that he does? Aren't many like this?

The cost of holding the Phillips position about belief and understanding is an extremely high one, though this seems little appreciated. It is that if one does hold this view, one loses a certain objectivity in thought and language, and so one inhibits philosophical discussion of religion. For on this position one cannot discuss religious issues indifferent to the question of whether or not the participants in the discussion are believers.

---

[10] Cited by Phillips, *Faith and Philosophical Enquiry*, 22.

So I shall assume in what follows that faith in God is faith in a matter of fact, which can be expressible in propositions, and which can be understood without believing the truth of that proposition. What is true of faith in God is also true, I hold, for any other propositions which may be objects of religious faith.

The *fourth* inhibitor of the philosophical discussion of faith that I shall discuss is the denial of objectivity just noted. The claims made by a theist are, if they are true, true for anyone and everyone. They are not simply true for the theist, or for those who join him in his belief, nor are they true because theists want them to be true, or because they have decided that they are true. If they are true then they are true whether anyone knows that they are true, or not, and whether anyone likes it, or not. This seems to be more obviously true of claims that God exists than of claims about the existence of some physical object. For it is part of the concept of God that he exists (if he does) necessarily, and that physical objects exist contingently. So the reality of God seems better entrenched than the reality of physical objects.

Thus religious belief, like any other belief about anything, has a stake in the truth; it occupies, in that sense, an exposed position. Defences of the intelligibility or reasonableness of religious belief ought not to have recourse to any version of subjectivism or relativism or communitarianism to limit or remove that exposure, tempting though such a move might be. And because religious belief has a stake in the truth, those who articulate their faith have a strong motive to get at the truth, to investigate, to think, to hypothesize, to consider objections, to engage in reformulations of the truth, in order to become as clear as they can about what it is that they believe; what it implies and what it does not imply.

I put the point in terms of theism; the same could be said of Christianity or of any other developed religion. Hard though it may be to live with the consequences, there is nothing to be gained from denying what is obviously true, that while the major (and minor) religions may share points of agreement, they make rival and incompatible truth claims.

The *fifth* inhibitor of the philosophical discussion of faith is the dogmatic claim[11] that religious beliefs are exempt from the demand

---

[11] It is necessary to distinguish a dogmatic and a reflective form of such a claim. Reasons may be offered why religion is exempt from such demands. This claim, like all philosophical claims, may warrant further discussion. Unreflective dogmatic claims of any kind obviously inhibit philosophical discussion.

of reasonableness; the question of the reasonableness or otherwise of a religious belief can never arise. This is a particularly difficult claim to handle because the notion of reasonableness is so slippery. There is, in considering the reasonableness or otherwise of a belief in a religion, the danger of making too stringent demands, the danger of being Procrustean. There is also the opposite danger of blessing manifest irrationality in the name of religion. But in what follows I shall be arguing for what at this stage might be called a minimum condition of reasonableness, that a religious belief is reasonable when it has relevant features in common with other beliefs taken to be reasonable. It seems to me that this minimum condition of reasonableness is not met when theologians claim that no reason can or need be given for, say, accepting something as a revelation from God. Keith Ward is surely correct in saying,

One need not be able to articulate all one's reasons for belief; it would be very rare to have that ability. But there must be reasons, factors which make it reasonable to believe as one does. That is what the theologian needs to spell out—the factors which make it seem reasonable to accept something as a Divine revelation. Barth and Brunner may be right in holding that there are no neutral reasons, which all rational persons can agree upon, for assenting to Christian (or any other) revelation. But they are wrong to draw the further conclusion that there are no factors which make it reasonable to accept something as a revelation at all. They may think that thereby they are freeing God's word from the tyranny of human pride; but in fact they are making it impossible to discover where God's word is to be found, amongst the many claimants to that status.[12]

And what is true of claims to revelation is true of other religious or theological claims.

As the language in which the Christian faith is presented is not some esoteric, private language, but the natural language which we all speak, so the standards to which it must appeal are general standards, standards applicable to any rational activity which makes comparable claims to those that the Christian faith makes. Of course if Christianity or some other religion make unique claims, then we might expect these general standards of reasonableness to have a unique application in such cases. And this possibility can be a source of much contention. Nevertheless, in considering the logical and epistemological character of Christian theism we need to appeal to what is reasonable, to general standards.

[12] Keith Ward, *Religion and Revelation* (Oxford, 1994), 18.

Besides the usual formal requirements of logical consistency, the following seems to me to be an axiom of rational belief: that the sort of evidence or reasoning for a particular belief or set of beliefs that may reasonably be required depends on the sort of propositions being considered for belief. It is unreasonable to expect the kind of evidence or reasoning which may be appropriate to establishing the rationality of belief in one kind of proposition in respect of another kind of proposition; and the degree of evidence appropriate to one kind of belief in respect of another kind. It is fundamental to the consideration of the rationality of a belief that an investigation into the truth of a claim, the evidence that is considered relevant, should be conditioned by the type of claim that is being made.

It may not be easy to distinguish between the level of evidence that it is reasonable to require, and the type of evidence. For example, consider the evidence that it is reasonable to require for belief in the presence in one's locality of an object that is inert in comparison with that required for something which has a measure of autonomy. Is this difference one of level or type? If one is content with making the sort of enquiries appropriate for something inert in the case of something with autonomy, one might end up with an unreasonable measure of scepticism about the existence of the putative autonomous individual.

In his essay 'The Will to Believe' William James states the following principle:

A rule of thinking which would absolutely prevent me from acknowledging certain kinds of truth, if those kinds of truth were really there, would be an irrational rule.[13]

If we understand 'kinds of truth' as truths about different kinds of thing then this, the James Principle as I have called it, seems eminently reasonable, and I will appeal to it a number of times in subsequent chapters. The Principle is important because it nicely balances a priori and a posteriori considerations that are relevant in the pursuit of the truth of some matter. It is important to keep an open mind, and not an empty mind. An open mind is one that is sensitive not only to general canons of rationality or reasonableness, but also to the unique features of what is being enquired into.

---

[13] William James, 'The Will to Believe', in *The Will to Believe and Other Essays* (New York, 1917), 28.

So, in summary, if the philosophy of religion is to be worth the name then the claims of religious faith must be open to philosophical scrutiny like any other claims. However, the privilege that a philosopher has of freely ranging over the issues raised by a religion or a religious tradition carries some responsibilities, the responsibility of informing himself of the doctrines and practices of the faith in question and of the sort of epistemic claims being made for them. Just as a political philosopher needs to know something about politics, and particularly about political theory, so a philosopher of religion needs to know something about faith, and particularly about the intellectual spine of any religion, its theology. To my way of thinking the philosophy of religion and philosophical theology are two ways of saying the same thing.

CONCEPTS OF FAITH

But even if the philosopher of religion sets about informing himself of the particular tenets of a religion, he will quickly discover that one other matter which inhibits the philosophical discussion of religion is the multiplicity of concepts involved in it. Nowhere is this truer than in the case of faith, even where we restrict attention to those kinds of faith which are doxastic in character.[14] What, as philosophers of religion, are we to do in this situation of conceptual plenitude? It is tempting to stipulate, to say that only one concept of faith is the correct or genuine one; and as we have seen, some, under the guise of describing the life of faith, do in fact make stipulations about it, or so it seems to me. Another temptation is to acquiesce in this pluralism by arguing that no one concept is to be preferred to another, and to be content with a purely descriptive, taxonomic approach to expressions of religious belief.

As has already been noted we are focusing upon doxastic types of faith. In the remainder of this chapter, and as a further preface to the chapters that follow, I want to make a bold but I hope not a foolhardy suggestion about how to handle this conceptual plenitude.

[14] To follow the helpful classification of William Lad Sessions, there are six models of faith: as personal relationship, as belief, as attitude, as confidence, as devotion, and as hope (*The Concept of Faith*, ch. 2). It is part of my argument that these models are not all exclusive of each other.

Prima facie, doxastic faith can be analysed into two types of doxastic elements, which nevertheless function differently. In the case of the first type of doxastic element, faith is solely a function of belief, and is therefore involuntary. The second type of doxastic belief concerns beliefs about what the believer wants, his goals and ideals, and the means to gaining them. In so far as these goals and ideals are chosen, and are not involuntary, this further doxastic element of faith will be more readily subject to the will. So the element of belief in faith includes not only beliefs about matters of fact but also beliefs about certain goods, and beliefs of a practically rational kind as to how these goods may be achieved.

So faith is strongly doxastic, involving beliefs about evidence and beliefs about ideals. How does the fiducial element of faith, that which distinguishes it from belief, arise? Belief becomes faith when, besides the presence of the various doxastic elements, the one who has these beliefs actually entrusts himself, relying upon the one the evidential beliefs identify and characterize, and engages in trust for the goods in question. The suggestion that I wish to make, and to argue for in the following chapters, is that of the two elements of faith, the doxastic and the fiducial, the doxastic element is primarily evidential (and involuntary), while the trusting that is exercised is primarily voluntary and capable of being morally assessed. For trusting is a disposition expressed in action, a disposition based upon a particular conception of the good. And so faith, including religious faith, has a peculiar combination of passivity and activity about it; its evidential aspect is passive, its fiducial element is active, and it is this active element which is sufficient to make faith an action. However, I shall not discuss the question of whether faith is a free action.

In emphasizing that trusting is an action, and that it has moral significance, I do not wish to imply that it has religious merit. For religious faith is not primarily trusting in order to bring about some change by acting, to accomplish some achievement, but primarily trusting as trusting to receive. The believer characteristically entrusts himself to God. It is this second sense, let us call it entrusting, that I wish to emphasize. It is a disposition, but it is not a praiseworthy moral achievement since it is not so much a doing as a receiving.

In order to illustrate the two sides of faith, the doxastic and the non-doxastic, let us suppose for the moment that some version of strong foundationalism is true, and that the existence of God is justified by reference to these foundations. That is, let us take it that there are optimal evidential grounds for belief in God. And let us further suppose that the believer has similarly strong reasons to believe that God is worth trusting. It does not follow from these two sets of facts, facts about evidence and facts about the worthwhileness of trust, that God will actually be trusted. Whether or not he will be trusted depends upon the will or endeavour of the one who has the evidence and who has made appropriate judgements about the worth of what there is good evidence for.

So for there to be faith in God two other factors are necessary besides evidence, so it seems to me. The first is the belief that there is something to trust God for; and then there must be the actual exercise of trust. To have faith in God, on this understanding of what faith is, is not to believe, against all the odds, that God exists and in addition to trust in him; it is solely to trust him on the basis of evidence and for the fulfilment of certain needs or goals. So having beliefs about X, even beliefs about X's trustworthiness, is distinct from trusting X. For even if trusting is primarily an action, the doxastic component of faith and the worthwhileness of faith do not ensure the occurrence of the action, since weakness of will may prevent this.

I shall spend some time on all of these points in subsequent chapters, but I shall bring this chapter to a close by saying something briefly about each of them. Trust in God is necessarily oriented to the future, though it may be based on what has gone before, on what God has promised, or even on something that is metaphysically necessary, such as God's immutability, which bears on the satisfaction of some need or desire that I have. The fact that there is good evidence that God exists, evidence of a foundationalist or some other kind, tells us nothing by itself about whether trust in God is warranted; that depends upon whether the person takes such evidence to be a good of sufficient strength to warrant the trust,[15] and whether God is a fit object of trust. For trust is non-contingently connected to some good, real or imagined. Suppose that what God promises me is heaven, and that like some other philosophers I find the prospect of heaven boring. In these circumstances it is not worth trusting God for heaven, and if I am consistent I won't trust him for it. I won't have faith in God for heaven, and if heaven is all there is to trust God

---

[15] And this may not be simply a matter of evidence, but also of the adoption of a policy about evidence. On this see Paul Helm, *Belief Policies* (Cambridge, 1994).

for, I won't trust God even though I may have good evidence both for his existence and that he promises heaven.

It might be argued that since trust is necessarily oriented to the future—one cannot now trust someone to have done something—and that as the past and present never entail the future, trust always goes beyond the evidence. But while this may be true in cases of trusting other people and trusting things such as suspension bridges, it is not obviously true in the case of the promises of God, whose omnipotence and immutability may be thought to provide a more than adequate link between the past, the present, and the future. Though here some caution is needed; while God's unchanging power may provide a link between present and future, the evidence upon which knowledge of that power is based is necessarily past and present evidence. This evidence gives grounds for trusting God's immutable power in the future, but if I am to similarly trust God tomorrow, then the evidence on which I trust him today must be available, in an unsullied form, tomorrow.

This view of faith, the view of faith which I shall try to develop in later chapters, may be contrasted with another, and perhaps (in the twentieth century) a more dominant idea of faith.

According to this concept of faith, faith is inherently risky, not because there is in fact little evidence and more would be desirable, but because evidence is in some way inappropriate for faith. Faith, at least in those areas of life where it ought to operate, supplants or expels rational belief, belief based upon evidence. Tertullian is reputed to have said that the death of the Son of God is certain because it is impossible.

According to another member of this family the strength of faith ought not to be proportional to the degree of belief, but it ought in some way to make up for the lack of evidence for the belief. This is Richard Swinburne's view in his *Faith and Reason.* Faith inhabits and flourishes in the atmosphere of evidential deficiency. I shall discuss this in detail in a later chapter.

In the case of yet another member of this family faith approaches knowledge, at least in some respects, but never becomes knowledge, not at least in this life. In the medieval period, in Thomas Aquinas, for example, a view of faith is developed in which faith falls short of knowledge (*scientia*) because many of the propositions of faith are incapable of demonstration, involving propositions which are mysterious and a matter of historical contingency, but which nevertheless carry the endorsement of the Church and so are utterly credible, with that degree of certainty but not that degree of explicitness which knowledge possesses. And even those propositions which are capable of demonstration, and so are capable of being demonstratively known, can be believed on faith, on the say-so of the revelation in the case of those who cannot follow the demonstration.

Kenny examines this view of faith, which he describes as follows:

> it is a belief in something as revealed by God; belief in a proposition on the word of God. Faith thus defined, is a correlate of revelation; for faith to be possible it must be possible to identify something as the word of God.[16]

Such faith

> was certain: it involved a commitment without reserve to the articles of faith; a resolve to disregard evidence conflicting with them. In this, faith was a state of mind resembling knowledge.[17]

Here, in Swinburne and Aquinas, we have two further members of the evidential deficiency family of views of faith, for each member takes faith to function primarily in an epistemic way. But in Swinburne's case faith makes up for the lack of evidence, while in Aquinas's case faith is held to be synonymous with 'strong belief', and the fiducial element all but disappears. Faith is certain belief in testimony. One trusts the testimony as one might trust one's senses, but one does not, characteristically, trust what the testimony testifies to, one believes it with utter certainty.

As I have already said, I wish in this book to propose and examine a view of faith that is distinct from this family of views, based upon a sharp distinction between the doxastic and the fiducial. On this view, for any person and for any proposition believed by that person there is some degree of evidence for (and against) that proposition. The strength of belief ought to conform to the evidence for the proposition in question, to seek to conform itself in strength to its reasonableness. It does not automatically conform itself, for there may be failure to perceive the evidence as a whole, by, for example, not appreciating the consistency of the set of one's beliefs about a matter. Such beliefs become apt material for religious faith when they include beliefs about God's ability to satisfy certain goals or needs. There may be degrees of such belief, depending upon degrees of evidence. And yet there is more to faith than sets of such beliefs.

---

[16] Kenny, *What is Faith?*, 47.   [17] Ibid. 49.

What more? There is trust. Thus faith is trust in the one who has promised or affirmed what is believed, and trust in that promise or affirmation. The difference between belief and faith is the element of trust, which relies upon the one for whom there is evidence for the conveying or realizing of some good. So while there is no conceptual connection between evidence which grounds the belief and beliefs about what is good for one (unless one subscribes to some form of ethical naturalism), there is a conceptual tie between the act of trusting and what is regarded as being good or important by the one who exercises trust, or would do so. Actual trust, as we have seen, requires strength of will.

On this view there may be faith in God where there is some evidence for the truth of what is believed in; some evidence that God exists; some evidence that he has promised certain things; and so on. The evidence may be great or small. But if the evidence is small then faith, reliance upon the one thus evidenced, cannot be entitled to be other than small or weak; if the evidence is greater, belief is stronger, and faith may be correspondingly strong.

CONCLUSION

Well, can religion be discussed? You would not expect me to have answered that question in the negative. I have tried to provide two sorts of positive answer to that question: the first is a set of general considerations, arguments rebutting the undiscussability thesis; the second is by actually beginning to discuss religion, one small but central aspect of it, namely religious faith.

In the next three chapters I shall try to say something on two current debates about the evidential side of faith, about the reasonableness of belief in God; and then, in subsequent chapters, to concentrate more attention on philosophical aspects of what in this chapter I have referred to as beliefs about goods that God can confer.

Faith and Foundationalism

The first chapter was chiefly devoted to the thesis that religious claims can be debated and discussed in philosophical vein in a similar way to, say, scientific or political claims. I then went on to distinguish two broad views of faith, which I call the *evidential deficiency* and the *evidential proportion* views. The evidential deficiency view sees religious faith, and particularly religious trust, as making up for gaps in the evidence for the religious claims believed by adopting a degree of certitude not warranted by the evidence. The evidential proportion view of faith sees the cognitive element in faith as being correlated with evidence: weak evidence, weak belief; strong evidence, strong belief. The believer should strive to conform the strength of his beliefs to the strength of the evidence for the proposition or propositions believed. But besides the beliefs arising from evidence there are beliefs arising from a person's awareness of his own needs and goals. These further beliefs turn the object of belief into an object of trust, though actual trust requires action beyond belief.

The two kinds of belief essential to faith (on the evidential proportion view) are capable of separate discussion. In this and the next two chapters I shall look particularly at the evidential beliefs, while in Chapters 5 and 6 we shall examine some elements of the fiducial and moral side of faith.

The question of the rationality of religious belief has recently been dominated by discussions of foundationalism and especially by the critique of strong foundationalism offered by Alvin Plantinga.[1] It is not my intention here to rehearse that critique in detail, but to discuss some of the features of one response to it, that offered by Anthony Kenny in *What is Faith?* I shall argue that it is possible to take account of Kenny's critique and still plausibly defend a form of

---

[1] I shall not in this book be considering Plantinga's later externalist turn in epistemology and its bearing on the rationality of religious belief.

foundationalism in which the proposition that God exists is in the foundations of one's noetic structure.

STRONG FOUNDATIONALISM AND ITS WEAKNESSES

The rationality of religious belief is often treated as if it were an all-or-nothing affair. Either religious belief is rational, or it is not. But the field of possibilities is much wider than this, and it may be helpful to sketch at least some of these possibilities as we start out.

First of all (though these points are made in no particular order) the criteria for the rationality of belief must be stronger, the stronger the degree of belief that is claimed. This is simply because a stronger belief has a higher cognitive stake than a weaker belief, since someone who strongly believes that p thinks that p has a higher degree of likelihood than if he weakly believes that p. So if for whatever reason one favours the view that religious belief is untentative, then the arguments offered in support of the rationality of such belief need to be correspondingly stronger than on the view that religious faith may involve belief that is highly tentative and qualified.

Secondly, the rationality of a belief may be distinguished from the epistemic justification of a belief.[2] Whether or not it is rational to believe a particular proposition depends upon what one already believes, so that it may be rational for one person to believe a certain proposition, and not be rational for another person to believe the same proposition. In this sense rationality is a 'person-relative' notion. To be able to display the rationality of one's belief is not necessarily to have justified that belief. The distinction between being rational and having a justified belief may be seen in the following way. Rationality is a property of people, and applies not only to their beliefs but also to their plans and actions. Rational beliefs are beliefs that a rational person has or ought to have; a rational action is one that is appropriate given a person's beliefs and desires. By contrast,

---

[2] For this distinction, see Robert Audi, 'Faith, Belief and Rationality', in James E. Tomberlin (ed.), *Philosophical Perspectives 5: Philosophy of Religion, 1991* (Atascadero, Calif., 1991). Despite this, in what follows I shall frequently use 'rational' and 'justified' interchangeably because the writers whose views I am discussing do so.

while rationality is concerned with the consistency of a proposition with a person's already-held beliefs, epistemic justification is concerned with establishing the credibility of a proposition or a set of propositions.

The distinction may be further developed in the following way. Rationality has to do with sets of concerns internal to the life of a particular person. Given that he believes such and such, then it may be rational that he believes so and so; if, say, that is consistent with the beliefs he already holds, and not obviously disconfirmed in current experience. Given that he believes so and so, it may likewise be rational that he endeavours to undertake actions of a particular type. At the heart of epistemic justification, by contrast, is some kind of universalizability. If a belief is justified for a particular person then the grounds of that belief are such that they are sufficient to justify any rational, open-minded person in adopting that belief when faced with the same evidence.

So given that the claims for justification are more stringent than the claims for rationality, irrationality is the worse noetic sin. Failure to justify a belief may be excusable when failure to establish its rationality may not. If religious faith involves belief in a weak and minimal sense, a sense which is more like the acceptance of a hypothesis, then showing the rationality of such belief is much less demanding than showing that a firm belief is justified. Perhaps some of the propositions of faith are strongly believed, others weakly believed. Then the criteria for the rationality of strong belief are correspondingly more stringent than those for weak belief. It is also worth pointing out that the rationality or irrationality of a religion involves wider sets of considerations than the rationality or irrationality of a religious belief. I shall return to this in Chapter 4. So much for these preliminary points.

Foundationalism is the view that lies at the heart of classical natural theology, and at the heart of foundationalism lies a principled contrast between those beliefs which are basic (because, for example, they are not inferred from any other propositions because they are evident to the senses) and those beliefs which are inferred from the basic beliefs. The relation between the basic beliefs of a person at some time and the non-basic beliefs of that person at that time is thus asymmetrical. If p supports q and r, then q and r cannot support p. And if S is the set of basic beliefs then any justifiable belief is supported by S. Foundationalism asserts that a proposition can only be justifiably believed if it is either (in Plantinga's terminology) 'properly basic' or suitably related to a proposition (or propositions) which are properly basic. We find such a view in Aquinas:

From effects evident to us, therefore, we can demonstrate what in itself is not evident to us, namely, that God exists.[3]

In this case the evident is what is foundational, the non-evident is what is inferred from what is evident. Aquinas attempts such demonstrations in his Five Ways, moving in typical foundationalist fashion from what is evident to us to what is not. Thus, it is evident to us that some things move, and from this (he believes) it can be convincingly argued that there must be an unmoved mover, God. Whether Aquinas also holds that it is *necessary* in order for faith to be epistemically justified that the existence of God can be demonstrated in this way, or merely *sufficient*, is an interesting additional question. To argue that the proofs are sufficient, but not necessary, would be to see Aquinas's use of the proofs as expressions of faith seeking understanding.[4] That is, Aquinas could be interpreted as offering the Five Ways as ways in which belief in God can be made evident, not as indispensable ways of justifying belief in God. On this view knowledge, *scientia*, is a luxury, not a necessity. However, to make matters simple, we shall assume that Plantinga is correct in claiming that Aquinas is committed to the necessity of the proofs for the epistemic justification of the proposition that God exists.

So let us suppose that Thomas, together with a host of other philosophers, argues that one is justified in believing that God exists only if there is evidence from which the existence of God can be derived. Or perhaps it is more accurate to suppose that he argues that one is justified in believing that God exists only if *someone* can derive the existence of God from evidence available to anyone. One's belief that God exists is not justifiable *without such evidence* but one may not need to provide the justification oneself. According to Plantinga, this means that Thomas must have a certain view about what constitutes a rational noetic structure, the structure possessed by the set of propositions that a person believes in so far as he is rational, together with all their logical connections. A rational person's noetic structure

[3] Thomas Aquinas, *Summa Theologiae*, *Part 1*, *Questions 1–13*, ed. Thomas Gilby (Garden City, NY, 1969), Ia. 2. 2, p. 66.

[4] For further discussion of this point see Paul Helm, *Faith and Understanding* (Edinburgh, 1997), chs. 1 and 2.

is constituted by a basis, his basic beliefs, together with what is built on this basis, the beliefs which are justified by the basic beliefs. Nothing justifies the propositions in the basis. It is only by coming to believe in accordance with such foundations that rationally justifiable beliefs can be formed. So Plantinga says,

According to the foundationalist a rational noetic structure will *have a foundation*—a set of beliefs not accepted on the basis of others; in a rational noetic structure some beliefs will be basic. Non-basic beliefs, of course, will be accepted on the basis of other beliefs, which may be accepted on the basis of still other beliefs, and so on until the foundations are reached. In a rational noetic structure, therefore, every non-basic belief is ultimately accepted on the basis of basic beliefs.[5]

One must not think of such foundationalism in too austere a fashion. The foundation may consist not of one or even of a few propositions but of sets of propositions, while the superstructure is (of course) built up by inference from such foundations. Nor is the relationship between the non-foundational propositions to be thought of in too linear a fashion. Non-foundational propositions may have strong and significant relations among themselves. For example, some superstructural propositions may be explained by others. The fact that I believe that I hear the wood-pigeon cooing, a non-foundational belief, is at least partly explained and justified by the belief that I see the wood-pigeon, another non-foundational belief. But if I am justified in believing what I see and hear this is due to the relation of these data to a foundational set of propositions in the manner already described.

So far we have thought of foundationalism chiefly as a type of structure of beliefs, some beliefs being basic, others being built upon and supported by these basic beliefs. *Strong* foundationalism is the view that a proposition is properly basic, properly among the foundations of a person's noetic structure, if and only if that proposition is either self-evident to that person or (less demandingly) evident to that person's senses. So on one interpretation of Aquinas, he was a strong foundationalist in respect of theology. To be strongly foundational a proposition must have such a character that it would be irrational for any rational person to deny it. So according to one dominant brand of strong foundationalism the superstructure of

[5] Alvin Plantinga, 'Reason and Belief in God', in Alvin Plantinga and Nicholas Wolterstorff (eds.), *Faith and Rationality* (Notre Dame, Ind., 1983), 52; italics his.

belief must be built upon propositions that are evident to the senses or which the mind has clear and distinct ideas of.[6] This is the dominant tradition in modern western philosophy, the tradition inaugurated by Descartes and Locke. Let us briefly consider Plantinga's critique of strong foundationalism.

Plantinga makes two criticisms of this view. The first is that it is too restrictive. For if strong foundationalism is true, then it rules out as irrational myriads of our beliefs; for example, beliefs about other people than myself, and about other times than the present, to look no further:

I believe, for example, that I had lunch this noon. I do not believe this proposition on the basis of other propositions; I take it as basic; it is in the foundations of my noetic structure. Furthermore I am entirely rational in so taking it, even though this proposition is neither self-evident nor evident to the senses nor incorrigible for me.[7]

There are two points being made here. One is that as a matter of fact there are many propositions which we believe, and are entitled to believe, which do not rest upon other, more basic propositions to make them rationally believable. Plantinga is making a move here that is typical of that type of epistemologist which Roderick Chisholm has called 'particularist'. He is appealing to particular examples of belief, noting their character, and in effect saying, 'If anything is a case of rational belief, this is. And so no theory or criterion of what rational belief must be like which calls the rationality of such beliefs into question can be warranted.'

The second point is that such propositions are to be believed even though they are *not* evident to the senses. In other words, strong foundationalism is unnecessary for epistemic justification. As far as I can see, Plantinga does not give an argument for this view, but makes an appeal to our normal procedures. He does not say that we cannot provide a justification for our everyday beliefs, but that we need not do so. (Perhaps he could appeal to a principle of credulity here.) We do not first have a theory, and then accept those beliefs which accord with the theory; we have certain beliefs which we take to be paradigmatically rational.

Secondly, and more seriously, Plantinga claims that such foundationalism is self-referentially incoherent. That is, it does not itself sat-

[6] Ibid. 59.
[7] Ibid. 60.

isfy the conditions it lays down for the rationality of any belief. It states that *a proposition is properly basic for a person only if that proposition is evident to that person's senses or is self-evident for that person.* But this proposition, the one that I have just emphasized, is itself none of these things. Strong foundationalism is an interesting philosophical proposal. It is one that many philosophers have accepted. But it is not self-evidently true and therefore we are not required, even as strong foundationalists, to accept it. The paradox is, no strong foundationalist need accept strong foundationalism. It is neither self-evident nor incorrigible nor evident to the senses.[8]

So *strong* foundationalism is indefensible as a necessary condition for rational belief. Though we may opt for strong foundationalism, there is nothing compelling about it. But as we noted, having rejected strong foundationalism Plantinga does not for this reason reject foundationalism in all its shapes and sizes. He reckons that our noetic structures do have a foundationalist character. But if strong foundationalism is not required, if it cannot be required for the reasons given, then other versions of foundationalism, if not required, are most certainly permitted. And among these other versions, according to Plantinga, is what might be termed *theistic* foundationalism. Plantinga holds that a person is entirely within his epistemic rights in believing that (say) God has created the world, even if he has no argument for this. The belief that God exists and has created the world can form part of the foundations of his noetic structure.

This is the claim which has provided the focus for much recent discussion on religious or theistic epistemology, and which lies behind Anthony Kenny's discussion, to which we now turn.

KENNY'S RESPONSE

Kenny is in agreement with Plantinga's principal point,

that it may be rational to accept a proposition though it is neither self-evident nor evident to the senses, nor held on the basis of any such reasons. There are many such propositions that I hold myself: such as, that I am

[8] Not all foundationalism is of that infallibilist variety which is open to the charge of self-referential incoherence. But then the initial attractions of fallibilism are not as great as those of infallibilism.

awake, that human beings sleep and die, and that there is a continent called Australia where I have never been; that there have been Christians for about two thousand years. I claim that I am rational in accepting all these propositions, and in no way guilty of credulity.[9]

But he proceeds to offer one basic criticism of this view, that it is too permissive. While it is rational to accept some propositions which are not evident to the senses, it is not rational to accept the proposition that God exists in such a way. For if one were to do this then that would open the floodgates. If one may accept 'God exists' why may not one, or why may not someone else, accept hosts of such propositions?

Plantinga has not shown us why what goes for belief in the proposition 'there is a God' may not go for belief in any proposition whatever. For all he has shown there would be nothing irrational in a noetic structure which included among its foundations 'there is no God'.[10]

Later on he avers that such a view as Plantinga's may be 'hospitable to lunacy'.[11]

Kenny may not be altogether fair to Plantinga here. For Plantinga counters the objection from permissiveness by making a distinction between *evidence* and *grounds*. Although a person need not have reasons (in the form of evidence) for his belief in God in order for that belief to be rational, nevertheless he would be irrational in his belief that God exists if that belief were not appropriately grounded. The groundedness of his belief that God exists shows that this belief is not arbitrary or whimsical. His belief in God arises from appropriate circumstances and occasions, and these situations provide the grounds for the belief. There is nothing extraordinary about this; a person is entitled in certain circumstances to declare that he sees a tree. But if he claims to see a tree when his circumstances do not entitle him to do so, then his belief is irrational. These circumstances ground his belief. But according to Plantinga these circumstances do not constitute evidence for his belief. Such a person does not need to have strong foundations for that belief to be rational; nevertheless this does not entitle him to go around declaring that he believes he sees trees when he has no grounds for such a belief. When he is not appeared to appropriately, then it would be absurd for him to claim to see them.

---

[9] Kenny, *What is Faith?* (Oxford, 1992), 13.   [10] Ibid. 13.   [11] Ibid. 20.

We must assemble examples of belief and conditions such that the former are obviously properly basic in the latter, and examples of beliefs and conditions such that the former are obviously *not* properly basic in the latter. We must then frame hypotheses as to the necessary and sufficient conditions of proper basicality and test these hypotheses by reference to those examples. Under the right conditions, for example, it is clearly rational to believe that you see a human person before you: a being who has thoughts and feelings, who knows and believes things, who makes decisions and acts.[12]

One may retort to this, as Norman Kretzmann has done,[13] that grounds are a species of evidence, and therefore that Plantinga's weak foundationalism is compromised. Or one might make the point that an atheist could also draw that very distinction, and thus maintain his atheism in a non-arbitrary way. Perhaps the atheist lacks sufficient evidence for his atheism but nevertheless has grounds for it. If so, he could maintain his atheism in a non-arbitrary way, and then it would be equally rational for *A* to be a theist and *B* to be an atheist.

Anyway, to cut a short story even shorter, Kenny offers his own criteria of rationality, a modified and somewhat complicated form of foundationalism. It is these criteria that I wish to examine, and then to look in detail at how they might be addressed by a foundationalist of Plantinga's stripe.

Kenny says:

A belief is properly basic, I claim, if and only if it is self-evident or fundamental—evident to the senses or to memory—defensible by argument, inquiry, or performance.[14]

These three criteria are meant to be applied disjunctively, I take it. That is, for a belief to be properly basic, it must be *either* self-evident or fundamental *or* evident to the senses or to memory *or* defensible by argument, enquiry, or performance. This is using 'properly basic' in a rather unusual sense, given that a properly basic belief is defined by Kenny (following Plantinga) as a belief in a proposition without evidence. Something that is evident to the senses or to memory is a belief that, normally, one would be said to have evidence for, the senses and memory providing evidence. And even if one accepts

---

[12] Plantinga, 'Reason and Belief in God', 76; italics his.
[13] Norman Kretzmann, 'Evidence against Anti-Evidentialism', in Kelly James Clark (ed.), *Our Knowledge of God: Essays on Natural and Philosophical Theology* (Dordrecht, 1992).
[14] Kenny, 'What is Faith?', 20.

Kenny's point that nothing can provide evidence for itself,[15] it is not obvious that using an argument to defend a proposition does not involve the provision of evidence. But we may let this pass. Kenny says of his threefold criterion that

It is a criterion which has none of the attractive simplicity of the foundationalist's canon of rationality. On the other hand it has one advantage over the foundationalist's canon: it is not obviously self-refuting as that one was. While this criterion is neither self-evident nor evident to the senses, it is not necessarily impossible to defend it by argument and inquiry.[16]

Self-evidence is a person-relative notion, as Kenny grants in his discussion of Plantinga. That is, what may be self-evident to one person may not be self-evident to another, so that the first clause of his criterion for rationality involves something like 'seems self-evident to *A*', where *A* is a rational person. This criterion may end up by having the sort of permissiveness which Kenny regards as such a weakness in Plantinga's theistic foundationalism. Because self-evidence is a person-relative notion, there seems no reason why Kenny can disallow the claim made by *A* that God's existence is self-evident to him. But Kenny's retort at this point that 'God exists' is not the sort of proposition that can possibly be self-evidently true to anyone. And this is his central contention against Plantinga.

He does not, as far as I can see, provide an argument for this contention, except by making a distinction between *self-evident* propositions and what he calls *fundamental* propositions. An example of a self-evident belief for Kenny is that Australia exists. This is a somewhat eccentric use of the term 'self-evident', for what Kenny means is something like 'undeniably obvious' and not 'knowable as true by examination of itself alone'. He says that he does not believe such a proposition on the basis of any reason because

If any of the 'reasons' for believing in Australia turned out to be false, even if *all* the considerations I could mention proved illusory, much less of my noetic structure would collapse than if it turned out that Australia did not exist.[17]

But surely we each have very many reasons for believing that Australia exists, so many that it is difficult to know where to begin in citing them. Perhaps if all these reasons proved to be ill founded, less

[15] Kenny, 'What is Faith?', 9.   [16] Ibid. 20.
[17] Ibid. 15; italics his.

of one's noetic structure should collapse than if it turned out that Australia did not exist. But not much less.

In any case what Kenny asserts here seems to be true of any conclusion about a belief concerning a matter of fact that one is asked to give evidence for. Less of one's noetic structure would collapse if one denied the evidence for a matter of fact than if one denied the matter of fact itself, since the evidence for a contingent matter of fact does not and cannot entail that fact. But Kenny must mean more than that a conclusion may have more purchase than its premises—he must mean that the very idea of proof would be overthrown if such a fundamental proposition were denied.

An alternative explanation would be to say that belief in the existence of Australia is part of a web of geographical and historical beliefs of such complexity that the few facts that one is able to cite do not by themselves entail or even render probable the belief that Australia exists. But this by itself is not an argument against Plantinga's foundationalism, or against certain other versions, because as we have noted it is consistent with foundationalism that one should acknowledge the interrelated, web-like character of non-foundational propositions. We shall look in more detail at the idea of a web of belief in the next chapter in connection with coherence theories of epistemic justification.

According to Kenny, by contrast to basic beliefs, which are relative to persons and times,[18] fundamental beliefs are 'beliefs which are basic in the noetic structure of every rational human being'.[19] Given that his criteria are offered as an account of rationality, this statement has the whiff of circularity or at least of inapplicability about it. For how can we decide which human beings are rational except by the application of the criteria in the first place? The criteria are intended to enable us to distinguish rational human beings from the rest. But perhaps we ought not let this danger of circularity detain us.

Kenny takes as an instance of a fundamental belief Wittgenstein's example 'The earth has existed for many years past' and Kenny himself offers the example 'Human beings sleep.' Kenny contends that while reasons can be given for these propositions, we do not believe them on the basis of such reasons, but take them to be fundamental. What makes a proposition fundamental is not merely that it is basic (as the belief that there is writing on the computer screen in front of

---

[18] Ibid. 16.   [19] Ibid. 21.

me now is basic for me) but that so much turns on it: if it turned out to be false, then giving it up would wreak havoc in our noetic structures. For truly to give up, or seriously to question, the proposition that human beings sleep would be to throw doubt on the reliability of the very processes of enquiry. For if one cannot believe a proposition such as that some human beings sleep, what can one believe?

When Kenny applies this criterion to the case of belief in the existence of God, he claims that belief in God cannot be fundamental, 'in the sense of being something that is accepted as basic by all those who have an opinion on the matter'.[20] 'While it is possible for an individual to accept the existence of God as basic . . . it is equally clear that the existence of a God with attributes resembling those of the God of Western theism is not something which has been universally believed by the human race.'[21] It is therefore not a fundamental belief. It is not universally believed, and therefore cannot be a fundamental belief in the required sense. This seems to be the argument.

But at this point, I think, we may need to make a further distinction. 'Fundamentally basic'[22] is ambiguous. In the first place it can be taken in a distributive sense, as a remark about the belief structures of everyone. When taken in this sense, it is doubtful if there is a common set of fundamental beliefs (in Kenny's sense) held by all intelligent and perceptive human beings, universally believed by the human race. Take, for instance, the claim that Australia exists, or that the earth has existed for many years. I suppose that not every intelligent and perceptive human being who has an opinion on the matter of the existence of Australia or the age of the earth holds that Australia exists or that the earth has existed for many years. 'The earth is approximately spherical' seems another good candidate for a fundamental proposition, but I don't suppose that all intelligent and perceptive human beings at present believe that the earth is approximately spherical, and in any case this seems to be a belief that has only fairly recently been acquired by most human beings. So there are very few, if any, universally basic propositions.

And certainly Wittgenstein, to whom Kenny is indebted for the idea of a fundamental belief, did not think that in order for a proposition to be fundamental it must be held by everyone in an unvarying fashion. For Wittgenstein held that 'The same propositions get treated at one time as something to test by experience and at another

[20] Ibid. 34.   [21] Ibid. 35.   [22] Ibid. 22.

as a rule of testing.'[23] So a fundamental belief for Wittgenstein is always a fundamental belief held at a time. Hence there is some confusion here about whether a fundamental belief can play the role Kenny assigns to it.

But 'fundamentally basic' could be taken in a non-distributive sense, taken to refer to the noetic structure of some individual human being such as you or me. There are no doubt beliefs in each of our noetic structures which were we to give them up, because we were persuaded that they were false (though how we could be so persuaded is a problem), the result would be the creation of havoc in our noetic structure. Perhaps for most of us belief in the existence of Australia is one such belief. But there is nothing in what Kenny says to stop the proposition 'God exists' functioning as a fundamental proposition in this, the non-distributive sense. For it is surely a fact that while for many people the existence of God, even if they believe it to be a fact, is non-fundamental in this sense, for many others theistic propositions are fundamental, basic not only to their noetic structures but to their entire way of life. It is not that were such a person to doubt the existence of God he would as a direct consequence doubt the reliability of his senses, since God is not an empirical entity. But it is possible that in doubting the existence of God one might doubt the reliability of one's intellect. A certain kind of Anselmian might hold such a position and, to look no further, though Descartes did not hold that the existence of God was clearly and distinctly perceived, and so the proposition that God exists does not figure in the foundations of his noetic structure, he certainly held the view that without the belief that God exists he could not trust the evidence of his senses. Acceptance of the existence of God was fundamental to his having a good reason for forming beliefs about the external world on the basis of what his senses told him.

Kenny's argument against God's existence being fundamental is that such a belief is not universal, both in the sense that not all believe in God in this fundamental way, and also that not all who believe in God believe in him in this fundamental way. But as we have seen, this can hardly be necessary for a belief's being fundamental.

Kenny offers a further argument, that the belief that God exists does not have the unshakeability characteristic of fundamental beliefs.[24] That is, it is not the kind of belief which can only be called

---

[23] Quoted by Kenny, ibid. 23.   [24] Ibid. 35.

into question by something which, in calling the belief into question, also calls itself into question. This follows without separate argument if what Kenny has just said is true. But this does not seem to be necessarily so.

God's existence is certainly highly unusual. If belief in his existence functions as a fundamental belief in Kenny's sense it can hardly be compared to the ways in which other beliefs function as fundamental beliefs. It is true that God does not figure as a hypothesis to solve empirical or scientific problems. But then, this is perhaps because he is not that sort of entity, and does not have that kind of fundamental character. The existence of God is not the existence of some entity in space and time. The existence of God, if is true that he exists, is, ontologically speaking, the basis of all other truths about the creation, at least all contingent truths; for it is in virtue of his deciding to create the universe, and creating it, that there are such truths. *Belief* in the existence of God may not be the epistemic basis, or one epistemic basis, for the many other propositions which we believe with varying degrees of commitment. But it is not, as far as I can see, part of what Kenny means by a fundamental proposition that it is the epistemic basis for *all* other propositions, not even for all other empirical propositions; this cannot be, if Kenny allows that there are several different and otherwise unrelated fundamental propositions. Kenny means only that the fundamental proposition in question serves as a foundation for a significant part of a person's noetic structure. And for many believers, though not of course for all, the existence of God most certainly does that.

But it may be replied that what has just been said does not quite answer Kenny's argument in favour of fundamental truths, which is that the denial of a fundamental truth is such that the very idea of there being evidence at all for it is called into question.[25] Hence any fundamental truth is unshakeable. But it may nevertheless be that someone who holds that God is the ontological ground of all other being, the creator of all that exists, would not be able to trust his senses were he not first convinced of God's existence. As we suggested earlier, was this not Descartes' position?

But could the belief that God exists function as fundamental in the sense that it is that kind of belief which can only be called into question by something which is in turn called into question?[26] Is it a belief

---

[25] Ibid. 17.   [26] Ibid. 35.

like Kenny's example, 'Human beings sleep'?[27] This is a belief such that were I to attempt to call it into question, then I could not trust the very process by which I called it into question. Any candidate for being a reason for disbelieving the belief in question would be something which called in question the possibility of there being any such thing as evidence at all. But of course the example is an empirical example; though one may believe such fundamental propositions without evidence, a suggestion which may seem to be rather implausible, nevertheless such beliefs are, we may say, evidence-pertinent, in that they implicitly lay down standards regarding good and bad evidence for other empirical propositions. One might be tempted to think that one can believe in Australia without evidence, but one could hardly believe that Brisbane is in Australia without evidence. And the evidence supporting the claim that Brisbane is in Australia may be part of the evidence that Australia exists.

Since God's existence is manifestly not an empirical matter of fact—though one might have empirical evidence for it—it could not be fundamental in the sense that 'Human beings sleep' is fundamental, but it may nevertheless be deeply embedded in a person's noetic structure. There may be other important matters, for example, objective moral truths, or that the future will resemble the past, or the miracle of the resurrection of Jesus, or life after death, which one could not rationally believe if God's existence is not fundamental. Of course not all these matters are important for everyone, but they are certainly important for some people.

So far we have seen that Kenny's first criterion, 'self-evident or fundamental', could be satisfied by a theist, provided that 'self-evident' is taken in a person-relative sense, and provided that we interpret 'fundamental' in a non-distributive rather than a distributive sense, and we have also argued that there are plausible reasons for such an interpretation.

Kenny's next criterion, 'evident to the senses or memory', can quickly be passed over. No theist claims that God is evident to her senses in any straightforward sense, nor to memory. As Kenny rightly says, 'If God is an immaterial spirit, and has no body, however ethereal, then God cannot literally be seen with the ordinary senses'.[28] I am inclined to agree with Kenny that the expression 'religious experience' has many different meanings and that it is difficult

<hr />

[27] Ibid. 16 f.   [28] Ibid. 38.

to understand the idea that a person might directly detect the presence of God by a religious sense in a way similar to those in which we detect the presence of physical objects by the use of our five senses. For this reason I have difficulty coming to terms with those versions of foundationalism which appeal to the experiential awareness of God as the grounds for having beliefs about God, such as that version propounded by William Alston.[29]

So let us look at Kenny's final criterion, 'defensible by argument or performance', which is, Kenny says, 'the most significant addition I wish to make to the foundationalist's categories of rationally basic beliefs'.[30] Here he makes a distinction between the reasons for which one believes *p*, the reasons why one continues to believe *p*, and the reasons by which the belief that *p* is defended; these may each be different, the point being that a belief may be held for no reason—Kenny cites his belief in Australia—and yet may be defensible to others by the giving of reasons.

Two questions arise, as Kenny notes: 'To whom is it to be defended, and how successful must the defence be?'[31] Let us look at these in turn.

Taken without qualification the idea of a rational defence by argument is a strong notion, containing at least three requirements. In order successfully to prove a proposition *p* by deductive argument, it is necessary that the argument be formally valid; that it be sound—that is, that the premises be true; and that it be convincing. That is, it is necessary that the person to whom one is defending the truth of *p* accepts that the argument is valid and that the premises are true. And correspondingly stringent requirements are necessary for inductive reasoning. The fulfilling of all these conditions is something of a tall order. Thus one may successfully defend the truth of a proposition without convincing someone else of its truth. In view of this it is not surprising that Kenny interprets the idea of a defence more weakly.

So let us consider his first question: Defend to whom? Here we are in danger of interpreting the criterion either too weakly or too strongly. To say that the defence can only succeed if it is successful against anyone looks too strong. No belief looks defensible on this view of what a defence ought to amount to. On the other hand, a stupid person may provide, as he thinks, a defence of his belief that is not acceptable to a wise and well-informed friend; and vice versa. So

---

[29] William Alston, *Perceiving God* (Ithaca, NY, 1991).
[30] Kenny, *What is Faith?*, 25.   [31] Ibid. 26.

narrowing down the particular target to whom the defence must be successful looks like providing us with too weak an interpretation.

Kenny himself says,

> For a belief to be properly basic for a believer B, B must himself be capable of defending it against those who are likely to challenge it. The believer's defence may take the form of referring the challenger to someone else who can conduct the argument or undertake the enquiry. But even in this case the believer must know who, or what kind of person, has the appropriate competence.[32]

Once again, it does not seem to me that the theist needs to despair in the face of this criterion of Kenny's. Many defences of theism can be mounted against various of its challengers, sometimes direct defences, sometimes defences which refer the challenger to an appropriate expert or authority. This conclusion is reinforced when we consider the question of how successful the defence ought to be to count as one. For Kenny says about the degree of success of a defence that it need not be so successful as to convince the challenger; he may be an unduly difficult person to convince, or perhaps the matter is one for which there is no knockdown argument. But the defence must produce evidence for the belief that is appropriate to the believer's degree of commitment. And it does not seem to be an unduly taxing matter for the theist to provide an argument or enquiry which need not convince a challenger but is one that is appropriate to the believer's degree of commitment.

Kenny later says that the existence of God can justifiably be held as basic, i.e. as a belief without evidence, if any of the traditional arguments for the existence of God can be shown to be sound and if the traditional arguments against the existence of God can be shown to be invalid.[33] These may be sufficient conditions of a belief's being a basic belief in Kenny's sense, but he has not shown that they are necessary conditions of rational belief. In the next chapter we shall consider another way of defending the rationality of religious belief.

As we have already seen, Kenny's idea of faith is that of a belief with that degree of strength akin to knowledge, a very high degree of strength, at least on one view of knowledge. (There are, of course,

---

[32] Ibid. 27.

[33] Ibid. 69. Kenny is using 'basic belief' here in a rather different sense than Plantinga: not as a foundational belief, but as one which the person who has it holds without question.

accounts of knowledge which do not entail certainty.) And so for someone with Kenny's view of faith it may not be an easy matter to provide an argument or enquiry which convinces him to the degree commensurate with that degree of strength needed for faith. But we need not accept this account of faith, as we have seen. If faith is capable of having different degrees of conviction, based upon the strength of the beliefs which accompany it, then it may be possible to provide an argument or enquiry which convinces a person to some degree, justifying him having faith to some degree. We shall return to this topic *con brio* in the next chapter.

So, what have we found? I have argued that there is nothing in Kenny's account of rationality that would prevent a theist holding the belief that God exists as a basic belief. That belief may be fundamental for him, and one that he holds with deep commitment, in that the proposition is deeply embedded in his noetic structure. He may not have reasons for it; nevertheless, he may be able to defend it by argument to the extent that Kenny's account of such a defence requires of him—to defend it against those who are likely to challenge him, with a defence that, though not necessarily convincing to every challenger, undercuts the objection.

So Kenny's account of rationality contains nothing that counts decisively against the rationality of belief in the existence of God as a fundamental belief. Thus it is possible to defend the rationality of a form of weak theistic foundationalism against Kenny's strictures.

FOUNDATIONALISM AND BEYOND

As we have noted, both Plantinga's defence of the rationality of theism, and Kenny's response to it, are examples of foundationalism. They assume that some form of foundationalism is the way to defend the rationality of belief, including religious belief. The chief argument for foundationalism is either a rational consensus argument, or the argument that rational noetic structures just are of this form, perhaps appealing to the fact that foundationalism terminates the regress of justification, thereby avoiding the circularity which threatens coherentism. This type of argument has certain advantages. Foundationalism is a clear, well-honed intellectual structure of general scope. The idea of basic or foundational propositions and a superstructure built on that foundation via deductive and inductive links is easily understood, and appealing.

But one needs to distinguish between foundationalism narrowly conceived, and variations on the foundationalist theme. Narrowly conceived, foundationalism is the view that there is a set of beliefs which are non-inferentially justified, to which all other justified beliefs are suitably related. Such foundationalism has often been linked to a particular view of natural theology. Let us call it the linear view. On this view (in the case of strong foundationalism), from certain foundational propositions it is possible to deduce or provide sound inductive support for the proposition that God exists. Then from the foundational propositions, together with the proposition that God exists, other theological conclusions are derived, and so on. In the case of weak foundationalism, the proposition that God exists already appears in the foundations, and so no separate step from a non-theological set of propositions to the proposition that God exists is required. But a linear strategy of arguing for further theological conclusions may still be adopted.

In such linear accounts of the rationality of religious belief the order of rational or epistemic dependence reflects closely the order of logical dependence. The proposition that God exists, on which the whole religious scheme logically depends, is that proposition which is given prominent attention either in the classical proofs of God's existence, or from its situation in a person's foundational beliefs, and it crucially figures as a premise from which all other religious or theological conclusions are drawn.

But is linear natural theology the best model for the rational justification of theism? Is it the best model for the rational justification of Christian theism? There may be reason to doubt that it is; it has at least three weaknesses.

First, linear natural theology has a strong tendency to be very abstract. In the case of strong foundationalism the concept of God presupposed is the God of natural theology, a being of supreme power, a first cause. In the case of weak foundationalism it is harder to generalize about the character of the God who appears in the foundations, for that may vary from case to case, since his presence there is warranted not by proof but because it is suitably grounded. And the God who is suitably grounded for one person may have a different character from the God who is suitably grounded for another. More on weak foundationalism in a moment.

Secondly, certain kinds of foundationalism are notoriously weak and implausible in justifying the crucial move from the existence of God to the existence of a revelation, a move that is clearly necessary in the task of grounding Christian theism in foundationalist fashion.

To take a recent example of a foundationalist who appeals from the existence of God to the existence of a revelation, in the course of a few pages in his treatment of revelation,[34] Richard Swinburne tells us that if there is evidence which makes it quite likely that there is a God, all powerful and all good, who made the earth and its inhabitants, 'then perhaps it becomes to some extent likely that he would intervene in human history to reveal things to them'.[35] He goes on to claim that it is obvious that human beings should have the opportunity to choose for themselves whether or not to make themselves fitted for heaven; it is good that we should be able to help each other in forming our characters;[36] there is reason to expect that God will take steps to ensure that men acquire information as to how to attain certain kinds of well-being;[37] it is good to have true beliefs about important matters;[38] it is good that men should have the opportunity to help each other towards material and spiritual well-being;[39] it is good that the revelation be something which they can help each other to find;[40] it is good that the revelation should not be too evident, even to those who have discovered it.[41] The appeal to these auxiliary propositions reads remarkably like a piece of special pleading. Although intended as an a priori argument for the likelihood of a revelation, it appears to be a piece of rationalizing after the event. However, it may be that there are more convincing ways of making the move from God's existence to the existence of a revelation, though it is hard to see how one could argue thus in the case of the extraordinary claims made in the Christian revelation.

Thirdly, linear natural theology does not do justice to the sort of centrality that God has in the narrative of the Christian faith. For the centrality of God in that narrative is not that he is separately demonstrable as a necessary being, but that he is the central character in a drama, the character in the drama who gives point to the whole, and who renders intelligible the actions of the other players in the drama. A linear natural theology is ill adapted to do justice to the intelligi-

---

[34] Richard Swinburne, *Revelation: From Metaphor to Analogy* (Oxford, 1992).
[35] Ibid. 69.   [36] Ibid. 70.   [37] Ibid. 72.   [38] Ibid. 73.
[39] Ibid. 74.   [40] Ibid.   [41] Ibid.

bility of a narrative, and narrative is central to the intellectual form of Judaeo-Christianity.

That linear natural theology is not entailed by foundationalism, and certainly not by the weak foundationalism of Reformed epistemology, can be seen by the sort of case Plantinga has in mind of how a religious belief is typically grounded.

Upon reading the Bible, one may be impressed with a deep sense that God is speaking to him. Upon having done what I know is cheap, or wrong, or wicked, I may feel guilty in God's sight and form the belief that God disapproves of what I have done. Upon confession and repentance I may feel forgiven, forming the belief that God forgives me for what I have done. A person in grave danger may turn to God, asking for his protection and help; and of course he or she then has the belief that God is indeed able to hear and help if he sees fit. When life is sweet and satisfying, a spontaneous sense of gratitude may well up within the soul; someone in this condition may thank and praise the Lord for his goodness, and will of course have the accompanying belief that indeed the Lord is to be thanked and praised.[42]

One may wonder how the grounds cited by Plantinga can be non-inferential in character. Indeed, perhaps Plantinga's words here ought to be interpreted as being favourable to a kind of coherentism in the justification of religious belief, despite his declaration to the contrary. While according to Plantinga propositions such as 'God is merciful to me' ground belief in God in foundationalist fashion, they may be propositions which are more susceptible to coherentist forms of the justification of religious propositions rather than linear justification. Nevertheless, though perhaps hospitable to a considerable degree of coherentism, the basic distinction between foundational and non-foundational propositions in Plantinga's account remains.

In making the suggestion that linear natural theology is inadequate I do not want for one moment to suggest that God is not a necessary being or that proofs of his existence have no place, but to make the point that emphasizing this necessity as a fundamental, logically or epistemically primitive fact does not begin to do justice to the place that God has in a developed religion such as Christianity. And we must, in accordance with the James Principle which I outlined and defended in the first chapter, be wary of adopting any ideal of rationality which prevents us acknowledging certain kinds of truth, if those kinds of truth are really there.

---

[42] Plantinga, 'Reason and Belief in God', 80.

In the next chapter we shall explore the idea that a better model for the consideration of the rationality of Christian theism is to think of it as a web of propositions in which there is no principled distinction between propositions which are foundational and the rest. The idea of a web of belief may provide us with a more plausible account of faith. In the first chapter, in looking at various concepts of faith, we saw reason to doubt Kenny's claim that faith must be thought of as a mental state of certainty akin to knowledge, while not being knowledge, and claimed rather that faith is, epistemically speaking, a much more variegated attitude, varying in its strength according to the degree of evidence possessed by a believer. If Kenny is correct then no matter how far away from the foundations a belief is, it should nevertheless be held with the same degree of certainty as one which is near the foundations, and this seems unreasonable. It is surely more realistic to suppose that the belief that certain propositions of a religion are true may vary enormously in strength and weight from belief in certain others.

So in the third and fourth chapters we shall attempt to bring aspects of the arguments of the first two chapters together in examining the idea that the rational justification of the theology of Christian theism is best accomplished by thinking of the corresponding religious beliefs as forming a web of belief, the justification of which may be best thought of as a case of coherentism in epistemic justification.

3

The Web of Belief

In the previous chapter we discussed some aspects of the current debate about so-called Reformed epistemology. I argued that the weak foundationalism of Alvin Plantinga was defensible against at least some of the objections made against it by Anthony Kenny in *What is Faith?* It might be thought that the natural thing to do next would be to consider natural theology of the classical foundationalist kind, but I am going to resist this temptation, or at least I am going to resist it almost entirely. By 'classical natural theology' is meant the proving or rendering probable of some theological propositions such as 'God exists' from premises which are not theological and which are, in addition, acceptable to any, or almost any, rational person. Thus from the proposition 'Some things move' Aquinas sought to establish the existence of an unmoved mover, God. But I should make it clear that the reason for not wishing to say much about such natural theology is not that I think, in the manner of Karl Barth, that the God of natural theology is a false god. It is that such foundationalistic natural theology, linear natural theology as I have called it, stands or falls with the cogency or otherwise of the proofs of God's existence, and to examine such proofs one by one would require another book. In addition, as we saw earlier, such linear natural theology does seem to have certain structural deficiencies as the first move in any attempt to defend the reasonableness of belief in a developed religion such as Christianity.

STRATEGIC ORDER

Although there is a strong historical connection between foundationalism and what I have called linear natural theology the connection is only a logically contingent one; commitment to foundationalism does not entail the adoption of linear natural theology. So while the linear strategy is possible for a foundationalist it is not necessary, though a strong foundationalist may find it difficult to avoid elements of linearity.

By contrast, the strategy to be developed in this chapter is coherentist. Such a strategy is possible for a foundationalist, for as we saw in the previous chapter foundationalism may nevertheless contain large elements of logical and epistemic coherence; after all, what could be more coherent than a valid deductive or inductive relation between the foundational and the non-foundational propositions? So this chapter is not intended as a criticism of foundationalism per se but only of some versions of foundationalism or of some uses to which foundationalism is put.

That linear reasoning from a starting point in natural theology is necessary for making religious faith reasonable rests upon an interesting but disputable assumption, the assumption that the order of establishing the truth of a set of propositions must mirror the logical order of the set. It is this assumption, rather than the foundationalism of classical natural theology per se, which seems to me to be a mistake.

Consider the following set of propositions:

Smith's sins are forgiven.
Christ is the Redeemer.
God has revealed himself.
God exists.

In Christian theology each lower proposition is logically presupposed by the next higher proposition. Thus it could not be the case that God has revealed himself unless he exists; it could not be the case that Christ is the Redeemer unless God has revealed himself; not, at least, on the Christian scheme of things. (Though there could be something that looks very like revelation from God were there to be a God and he reveal himself. That is, it could be that something so extraordinary or so morally sublime occurs that it is judged to be an appropriate vehicle of revelation were God to exist, and even to provide an argument for his existence.) And finally, it could not be the case that Smith's sins are forgiven unless Christ is the Redeemer. The fundamental break, for our purposes, is between the lowest proposition in the list, and the remainder. For clearly if God does not exist then nothing can be true of him. Let us call 'God exists' a level one proposition, 'God has revealed himself' a level two proposition, and so on.

It is tempting to assume that the project of enquiring into the reasonableness of a developed religion such as the Christian faith must follow the logical order of the key propositions or claims of that religion; that because 'God exists' is the fundamental proposition in any theology the truth of that proposition must be the first proposition to be established by argument. Only when the proposition that God exists has been established as a reasonable belief would it make sense to proceed to propositions which logically presuppose the existence of God and to attempt to establish the reasonableness of these, by appealing not only to whatever is evident to the senses (or to what is in some other way reasonable) but also to whatever is evident to the senses together with what has already been established, namely that God exists. Having established the reasonableness of level one propositions it is then reasonable to proceed to level two, and so on to propositions of succeeding levels.

On this scheme of things, having established the reasonableness of God's existence the next move is to look for certain signs which make it reasonable to believe that a particular document or some other source of information is God's revelation. So Aquinas invites us to place our confidence in Scripture as the word of God because its truths are confirmed miraculously:

There are the wonderful cures of illnesses, there is the raising of the dead, and wonderful immutation of the heavenly bodies, and what is more wonderful, there is the inspiration given to human minds, so that simple and untutored persons, filled with the gift of the Holy Spirit, come to possess instantaneously the highest wisdom and the readiest eloquence.[1]

But what is the argument for the claim that the order in which one attempts to establish the reasonableness of a faith must follow the logical order of the constituent propositions of that faith? On reflection this looks to be an unnecessarily demanding requirement. Suppose I show you a box, but that you are too far away to see inside it, and that you are sceptical about my claim that there is something in the box. And suppose that what I have in the box is a grass snake. There is no reason why I should first attempt to prove to you that what I have in the box is a physical object, and then that it is animate,

[1] Thomas Aquinas, *Summa contra Gentiles*, i, trans. A. C. Pegis (Garden City, NY, 1955), I. 6. I.

and then that it is reptilian, and so on. Nothing can be a grass snake if it is not a reptile, and nothing can be a reptile if it is inanimate, but this logical ordering of properties does not require that the evidence for some object should follow the logical ordering of its properties in parallel fashion.

This is not how we in fact proceed in learning about things around us, the only notable class of exceptions (perhaps) being certain kinds of forensic investigation. Not even small children learn in this step-wise fashion. Besides, such a procedure depends upon the teacher knowing all members of the logical hierarchy, for if through igno-rance or inadvertence he misses one out then the argument could not proceed, since the teacher could not move to the next logical level until the truth of the proposition at the previous logical level has been established.

Furthermore, perhaps the concept of God is much more like the concept of a carburettor or a liver than it is like the concept of a rock, say. Although one can identify something as a carburettor by its physical properties, assuming that all carburettors have a distinctive design, one cannot understand or explain a carburettor (or a liver) without reference to its role in a mechanical (or organic) scheme of things. And it may be that one way, perhaps the best way, of estab-lishing the rationality of belief in God is to show how the idea of God functions to integrate diverse data that are otherwise harder to explain. On this view one does not establish the rationality of belief in God as a separate exercise any more than one establishes that something is a carburettor solely by features which make no refer-ence to its function. It may be in introducing the existence of God as the explanation of diverse data, and as performing a distinctive role, that the rationality of belief in him is established.

Does this mean that linear natural theology has no uses? Not at all. To draw this conclusion would be unduly rash. Because such a strategy need not form part of the project of establishing the reasonableness of a belief it does not mean that it has no uses at all. Nor, as we have seen, does the fact that linear natural theology need not be used in the con-struction of apologetic strategies mean that reason should play no part in such strategies. Classical natural theology is an intellectual pro-gramme of surprising ambition, an attempt to establish by the most stringent intellectual standards that God exists. This does not mean that natural theology is a game. But nor does it mean that if as a result of some intellectual feat it were possible to establish the existence of

God by one or other of such purely rational means, then that result should immediately find its way into the apologetic armoury. Nor does it mean that failure to prove the existence of God by this strategy ensures that belief in God is unreasonable; this would be an unusually demanding requirement. It would be like supposing that the failure of arguments for other minds meant that it was unreasonable for me to think that you have a mind. Nevertheless, natural theology may have many uses; for example it may serve to strengthen the grounds that a believer has, to turn a good epistemic state into a better one.

In this chapter I shall be examining and exploring a mode of argument that accords better, it seems to me, with the overall claims and character of a particular, developed religion such as Christianity: the proposal that such a religion be considered, epistemologically speaking, as forming a web of propositions. Notwithstanding my defence of a form of foundationalism in the previous chapter, a version in which, as we noted, coherence in fact occurs, I wish now to take a further step and to argue that the reasonableness of a developed religion such as Christianity is best displayed if it is thought of as forming a web of beliefs in which there is no principled distinction between foundational and non-foundational propositions within the beliefs of that religion.

The contrast between foundation and superstructure is generally represented as between a set of non-inferential, foundational propositions, and a superstructure inferred from the foundation. Coherence theories deny this. Thus Laurence BonJour:

> The basic claim of a coherence theory of empirical knowledge is . . . that all of the warrant-increasing properties of empirical beliefs are ultimately inferential. A foundationalist theory, in contrast, must hold that there is at least one warrant-increasing property which is not ultimately inferential.[2]

So according to coherentist accounts of empirical knowledge there is no set of basic, non-inferential beliefs on which all other warrantable empirical beliefs are based; rather, whatever increases the justification of beliefs about matters of fact is inferential justification.[3] I wish

---

[2] Laurence BonJour, *The Structure of Empirical Knowledge* (Cambridge, Mass., 1985), 80.

[3] It does not follow that the justification of all propositions best follows one pattern. For it is entirely possible that of all propositions concerning matters of fact, the subsets of those propositions which are religious (and perhaps other subsets) are to be justified in coherentist terms, while perceptual beliefs (say) are to be justified in foundationalist terms.

to apply this pattern to the justification of belief in the propositions of Christianity.

The second thing implied in saying that religious propositions may (epistemically speaking) form a web is that while there is no principled distinction between non-inferential foundational propositions and the superstructure inferred from these, nevertheless certain propositions are more central than others. But such centrality is a matter of degree, and is a function of either the logical order and the explanatory importance of the propositions in question, or of both these things. If denying a proposition p has serious consequences for the truth of many other propositions, e.g. q, r, and s, but denying any of q, r, and s has consequences for few propositions, then we may confidently say that p occupies a more central position in the web than do q, r, or s, and so is of more cognitive importance. So coherence among propositions is more than consistency; it includes explanatory power.

The third point in emphasizing the web-like, coherentist character of religious propositions is that although some are more central than others, the web, like a spider's web, is characterized by the mutual support of all propositions within it, a support characterized by the power of some propositions to render other propositions intelligible and hence plausible. Belief in one or more propositions in the web causally sustains belief in others in the web, and so on in relation to all propositions in it. The lines of justification are not linear, nor do they run only from the centre of the web to its outskirts. So there is no danger of the regress of justification proceeding indefinitely, and therefore no need to invoke a non-inferential stopping place for such regresses. In coherentism justification is system; a proposition is justified by being related through inference to other beliefs in the system and they to it. Thus a peripheral proposition lends support to a central proposition in precisely the way a central proposition lends support to the periphery, but not of course with the same strength or intensity.

Coherence, as I am understanding it, is a degreed property of sets of beliefs for a person at a time. No doubt there are forms of coherence where this does not need to be stressed. But in religion many beliefs which form part of the web are person-relative beliefs, beliefs which other people do not share. Another person cannot now have those beliefs, or cannot at present hold those beliefs with a greater degree of strength than they in fact do. They could have had those beliefs had they previously come to hold different beliefs, and they may in future come to have them. So a set of propositions could be coherent for A at a time and not for B (or be less coherent for B) at that time, because A has beliefs in addition to the set which B possesses and fails to have some of B's beliefs, and as a result the set of A's beliefs is more coherent for A than the set of A's beliefs is for B and, of course, vice versa. The idea of person-relativity will be considered further in Chapter 4.

Thus what justifies the entire system of religious beliefs, the theology of a religion and all that is associated with it, is chiefly the coherence of the entire system of beliefs, where these beliefs may include person-relative beliefs. Individual propositions, in isolation, may be justified by the others in the set, but the set as a whole is chiefly justified by its coherence for a person. This does not mean that perfect coherence is ever attained, however. At any time there are numerous recalcitrant and otherwise ill-fitting propositions whose presence weakens overall coherence, while not leading to downright incoherence.

THE WEB

As we have already noted, the point of using the model of a web in connection with establishing the reasonableness of a developed religion such as Christianity is to stress three things: that all the various elements of the faith are interconnected; that these are mutually supportive (though they do not support each other in symmetrical fashion); and finally, that some elements in the web are more central than others, but no elements in the web are privileged in the way in which according to foundationalism some propositions are privileged, by being known non-inferentially.

I thus agree with Richard Swinburne when he says that

It is an integrated web of argument from the whole of experience which leads to the Christian doctrine of God; and that doctrine is justified to the extent to which that web is a seamless garment.[4]

The idea of a web of belief, when applied to Christian belief, is surely an initially attractive and plausible one. For if one takes a central

---

[4] Richard Swinburne, *The Christian God* (Oxford, 1994), 238.

Christian affirmation such as the Apostles' creed, one finds both that the propositions of that Creed are of diverse types, and that it is implausible to suppose that they are best understood in linear fashion, but should rather be construed as a narrative, a story with a beginning, a middle, and an end.

Thus the affirmations of the Creed involve the existence and character of God (including his trinitarian character), affirmations about what he has done as Creator, historical and empirical propositions about what Jesus Christ did and what happened to him (he 'suffered under Pontius Pilate, was crucified, dead and buried'), propositions expressing miracles (the resurrection of Jesus), statements about society (I believe in the Holy Catholic Church), and hopes and fears for the future (the second coming of Christ, the Last Judgement).

Not only is there this sort of connectedness, the sort that we are familiar with from historical and fictional narratives (about which I shall say more later), but there are also connections of various other types between many of the propositions in the web. Not only is there a causal connection between, say, the existence of God and the Incarnation, but there is also a relation of meaning. The Incarnation can only be *understood* in terms of the doctrine of God; the forgiveness of sins can only be understood in terms of propositions which imply the Incarnation; and so on.

A little earlier I argued that for a developed religion such as Christianity justification is chiefly, though not solely, a matter of coherence. It is important to see why this is.

Just as the Christian faith has metaphysical and logical assumptions, assumptions that it has in common with any other matter which claims a similar metaphysical and logical status, so also empirical assumptions lie behind some of its central claims. For example, while part of the web contains the proposition that Jesus Christ is the eternal Son of God made flesh—a profound metaphysical claim—another part maintains that Jesus was a palpable, historical person. He could be conversed with, seen, and touched. So if it is maintained that the very idea of an Incarnation is incoherent, or that there is very good evidence to show that there was no such historical person as Jesus Christ, then this is clearly relevant to the integrity of the web. Thus it is with propositions which are not intrinsic to the web of religious belief, but which have much greater generality. Historical and metaphysical propositions, for example, may bear upon the intelligibility and the credibility of the web as a whole. Whether these extra-web features are themselves part of the wider circle of justification along coherentist lines, or whether they are better justified in other ways, is for us a separate question. More on this later.

Here again, the analogy of a web is apt. Though the strands of a spider's web support each other, the web does not float in thin air but also has extra-web supports. The interconnections of the web of belief, its nodal points, are not generally formed by a relation of deducibility or of inductive probability; it is much too extreme even to suppose that any non-central proposition can be inductively supported by the central proposition, 'God exists'. There is a weaker logical relation which is more plausible: logical dependence. The less central propositions logically depend upon those that are more central. The central propositions are logically necessary conditions of the truth of the less central, but not logically sufficient. But this is not all there is to the interconnections, for each renders to the other segment a degree of intelligibility and plausibility; there is a relation of reciprocal explanation.

Some propositions are explained as being reasons for action, reasons for divine action, for example. If reasons are causes, these are causal explanations. But they might nevertheless not be explanations in terms of scientific laws, but personal explanations.

So a web, at least as applied to a developed religion such as Christianity, is more like a narrative, with central characters and some less central, and various settings where the action of those characters takes place. The story 'adds up' to the extent that the action of one character is intelligible in the light of the other features of the narrative, including the actions of the other characters. Though the doctrine of God is logically central, the intelligibility of assertions about the character of God depends upon other features of the web, and they upon it. For example, what is meant by the goodness or the power of God is not determined wholly a priori, by appealing to a set of abstract values, but only by reference to the other features of the web, assertions about what God has done and not done.[5] The other features of the web fill out the description of what kind of God the Creator is, even if they do not and could not complete the description.

The idea of a web of belief has one obvious attraction over the linear natural theology model in that it does not involve putting all its

[5] On this see Paul Helm, 'The Perfect and the Particular', Inaugural Lecture, King's College, London, 1994.

eggs in one basket. It is true that for some kinds of linear natural theology, the basket may be thought to contain numerous eggs also; there may be several foundational propositions, not just one. And it may be possible to repair a breach in the foundations by providing alternative foundational propositions, and a non-foundational proposition may have more than one foundational support. Nevertheless if the foundations fail, then the whole building collapses, as one would expect, unless alternative foundations can speedily be provided. In the web model, this is not the case; if there is good reason to doubt the truth of some more central proposition, then the remaining propositions may reinstate it. For on the model of the web epistemic order does not invariably follow logical order.

Further, I should like to stress again that the idea of a web of belief as I am proposing it is that of a *personal* web. It will be a web that one shares much of with others, but the precise character of the web, its exact shape and strength, depends upon personal judgements made about the elements of what is believed at that time, their coherence among themselves and with beliefs which, as we saw, lie outside the web of religious belief strictly speaking, and which form parts of other webs of belief, for example, geographical and historical beliefs. For better or for worse, it seems to me to be one of the abiding legacies of the Reformation for Christianity that religious faith is personal faith, the expression and working-out of a personal project. Even if one gives adherence to authorized interpreters of the faith, or has a high view of Church tradition, the *consensus fidelium*, or the authority of the Bible in matters of faith, each of these is a position which is nowadays a matter of personally acquired conviction, not of implicit faith or of universally accepted truth. The genie is out of that particular bottle and it is impossible to get him back in.

In the case of the Christian faith the exact character of such a web of propositions will inevitably be based upon hermeneutical assumptions about the canonical epistemic sources of the faith. A glance back at the history of the Church, and particularly at the history of biblical interpretation, shows that objections to the faith have repeatedly been the occasion of hermeneutical revision. The geocentric nature of the universe, a particular age for the earth, a particular quasi-scientific view of the origin of species—these are but examples of what people have from time to time taken Scripture to teach, only to have such views overturned by controversy in which the faith has been under attack. How do we know for sure that the presently held set of hermeneutical findings is the correct one? Clearly we do not.

No reasonable view of the reasonableness of religious faith can give immunity to this difficulty, for all strategies are ultimately cast back on some particular interpretation of the primitive faith. After all, in attempting to articulate the faith at any time one naturally assumes that there is something to articulate. As a result of controversy or of further independent reflection one may come to see that what forms part of one's personal web of belief now is different from what previously formed it; the transformation might even pass largely unnoticed. Ultimately, in this area as in any other area of human activity which requires thinking, a person must back his own judgement at a particular time, recognizing its fallibility, as well as the possibility that the appearance of new data will lead to further revisions in the future.

COHERENCE

As we have noted, it is implicit in the idea of a web of belief that coherence, both in the sense of logical consistency and of explanatory power, is to play an important role in the rational justification of many of our beliefs. Hence it is in accord with the reasonableness requirement outlined in the first chapter that coherence may play a role in the rational justification of religious belief, unless it can be shown that the propositions of a religion are not amenable to this sort of treatment. Some may voice the same objection to the coherence theory of epistemic justification as to the coherence theory of truth, that a set of propositions may be coherent but false. While this is a decisive objection to a coherence theory of truth, it is not a decisive objection to coherence as a defence of the rationality of belief. Our beliefs in such a complex of propositions may be rationally grounded but false, but this is the possible fate of a set of beliefs on any account of rationality unless every step is from self-evident foundations and is a self-evident step to take, and this is an unreasonably tall order. For what has in the past been taken to be self-evident has turned out not to be, and the present is no different from the past in this respect. A belief may be based upon what seems to be a set of self-evidently true propositions and yet turn out to be false. So it is perfectly true that a set of religious beliefs may be consistent but false, but then so may any set of propositions. Coherence as an epistemic principle must be distinguished from coherence as a criterion of truth.

Although in the last chapter we considered the question of the rationality of belief in God's existence as an isolated belief, according to the idea of a web of belief, belief in God does not have to be separately defensible to be rational; it is logically prior to certain other beliefs in the web, perhaps to all beliefs in it, but not necessarily epistemically prior, or not epistemically prior on its own. It may occupy the centre of the web, or part of the centre, but propositions on the periphery of the web may offer rational support for it, just as it offers rational support for them.

This sort of logical and evidential relationship is not peculiar to the role played in Christianity by the proposition that God exists. Consider memory. Our memories also form a web, perhaps a series of webs. Within each web are central facts, facts on which many other of our memory beliefs depend, and which provide some of the grounding for those beliefs. But on occasion a sufficient number of peripheral memory beliefs may also provide renewed grounding for more central memory beliefs which have suddenly come under suspicion. Suppose that we suddenly developed selective amnesia, and forgot some of our more central memory beliefs, or were overcome by sceptical doubts about them; then the remaining less central beliefs might provide grounds for rationally reinstating them. Hence the idea of a mutually supporting web of belief. Similarly, I shall argue, with Christian belief.

How might we express the nature of the interconnectedness of the web, its logical and epistemological character? In trying to answer this question, we must bear in mind the point which we touched on previously, that this web of belief exists in a more general framework of belief about other matters.

It is necessary to make a distinction between the central, core propositions of the Christian faith—those which are, in a sense, constitutive of it, and which have been repeatedly tested against the primitive documents and found to faithfully reflect their meaning—and those claims to which less certainty attaches, for which a greater refinement may be called for in future. That is, one must observe the James Principle to the extent of observing the web's estimate of itself, and not seek to impose an a priori pattern on it. Perhaps some doctrinal disagreements within Christianity can be understood in terms of different parties giving different positions in the web to the same proposition. One group may attach great importance to certain values, and see Jesus Christ as the paradigm exemplification of those values; others may attach priority to empirically testable truth; still others to certain basic ontological claims. So one must not be surprised to find a mixture of certainty and caution in beliefs in the web as a whole.

Further, there are many central features of the web of Christian faith which are extremely difficult to grasp because they are so remote from human experience, and so unparalleled in human affairs. We may consider, as an example, the issue of God and his relation to the created universe. What exactly is that relation? How does God sustain the universe? How is the fact that he ordains all events compatible with the free and responsible behaviour of those made in his image? How are the events of history, of divine providence, to be understood? The difficulties experienced in attempting to answer such questions are represented by gaps in the web of belief, and scepticism, if it arises, may prey on such gaps.

Can we be more precise about the character of the web? Let us make a rather rough and ready distinction between the *centre* of the web; the propositions which surround this centre, let us call them the *intermediate* propositions; and finally the *peripheral* propositions. We might say of the centre of the web that it consists of fundamental propositions which are a logically necessary condition for the truth of all other propositions of the web. These propositions carry the greatest logical burden and usually, but not invariably, the greatest epistemic burden. The intermediate propositions are a set of propositions, consistent with the central propositions and with each other, which elucidate and explain each other and provide support for the centre, while the centre provides support for them, and the detachment of any of them would diminish the intelligibility and plausibility of the remainder. These carry the next highest logical burden. Finally, the peripheral propositions are single propositions or small groups of propositions which are detachable from the central and intermediate propositions without diminishing the intelligibility and credibility of these propositions very much. These have the lowest degree of logical power.

This is a set of logical distinctions based upon the idea of logical dependence and importance. Set alongside this there are epistemic relations between elements of the web, which (as we have stressed) may not at all coincide with the logical relations. That is, it may be that the logically basic correlates with the evidentially central. What is, logically speaking, an intermediate belief may correlate with what there is next most evidence for. Alternatively, a person may be led by her belief in certain peripheral propositions to accept certain intermediate propositions as reasonable, and thence to accept certain central propositions. And along the way a certain amount of reinterpretation of the relevant data may take place.

To give an example, there may be good reason to think that the story of Jesus changing water into wine—a proposition on the periphery of the web, let us assume—is not likely to be true, perhaps on Humean grounds about the trustworthiness of reports about the miraculous. But other propositions in the web, propositions about the divinity of Jesus or the creatorship of God, for example, may provide reasons for having second thoughts. It is not sufficient for the credibility of the story that the account of the changing of water into wine is consistent with Jesus' divinity and God's creatorship. Rather, in this case the two more central propositions provide grounds that increase the credibility of the more peripheral proposition. It is a commonplace that the subjective probability and the plausibility of a belief depend upon what one already believes.

The overall rationality of the web of religious belief may also depend on evidence coming from outside the web, from other sources of belief. For as we have noted, the web of religious propositions is only a subset of all propositions which a person may believe. It is not necessary to my argument here to claim that these others all have web-like characteristics, for I am not here arguing for—or for that matter arguing against—a coherence theory of the rational justification of all propositions. But propositions outside the web of religious belief may either offer rational, say empirical, support in the case of empirical propositions in the web, or they may take away support from such propositions. A person may find intra-web support for a proposition, but no extra-web support; perhaps the extra-web evidence, considered by itself, is grounds for the negation of the proposition. Someone in this position is called upon to judge the rationality of believing the proposition in question given the balance of evidence and counter-evidence; the familiar interplay of theory and interpretation. So strong may be the logical and evidential lines binding one particular proposition into the web that it may be rational not to reject the proposition on the strength of the extra-web evidence, but to suspend judgement. Perhaps the rational thing to do in such a case is, as with certain scientific theories, to be tenacious over the integrity of the present shape of the web and to reinvestigate the grounds on which the extra-web claims for the falsity of the proposition are made.

So commitment to a proposition within the web carries responsibilities. For example, if the relevant web proposition is metaphysical in character, and if the believer appreciates arguments that are given for why such a proposition cannot be true, then there is a prima facie obligation on him to examine the arguments put forward for this conclusion. Such an examination would typically involve considering other elements in the web. If the relevant proposition is empirical in character, and the web is placed under strain by the serious claim that such an empirical proposition is false, then there is a prima facie obligation upon the one committed to the web to revise his position. There are various possibilities at this point; for example, to believe the proposition less strongly, to drop the proposition entirely, to give it a less central logical role, or to adopt the more drastic response of giving the words in which the proposition is expressed another meaning.

And so, bearing in mind what has already been said, that this web exists within a framework of other beliefs and perhaps of other webs of belief drawn from other areas of human enquiry (the extra-web beliefs), we may say that extra-web beliefs may both confirm and disconfirm web beliefs. For example, suppose the proposition that there is a Sea of Galilee is an extra-web belief and the proposition that Jesus taught by the Sea of Galilee is a web belief. The first belief, if well grounded, will provide some grounds for believing the second proposition. And the closer towards the centre of the web one travels, the greater the degree of tolerance there may be of extra-web evidence against; but there can never be total tolerance, otherwise one jeopardizes the cognitive status of the web as a whole. This is one reason why it is very difficult to sustain a position which makes no appeal, not even a tacit appeal, to any extra-web belief.

It is part of the character of such a web when applied to Christianity that there may be sets of second-order propositions within it. Thus, for example, not only are propositions asserting the providence of God part of the web, but there is also the proposition that God's providence is hard to fathom—that is also part of the web. That is, there are grounds within the web for thinking that other parts of the web are hard to understand. Again, part of the texture of the web may be that God brings about the unexpected; that there is no a priori likelihood in the choice of Abraham, or the occurrence of the Incarnation. And so another second-order belief in the web is the belief that the unexpected is to be expected. To expect the unexpected is not to do something which is incoherent; it is to adopt an attitude of readiness to have one's present expectations overturned. The dogmatic denial of the propriety of such second-order beliefs would be contrary to the James Principle.

Some second-order beliefs of this kind have to do with error. It is a fact that many people find the Christian web of belief less than fully rational, and hence not fully belief-worthy. But we may find within the web accounts of why this is. So the fact that B, an otherwise rational person, does not believe the web of propositions to be rational does not provide A with a strong prima facie reason for regarding the web of propositions as irrational. Why not? Because the web itself provides a reason why some otherwise rational people will not accept it—either through ignorance, or misperception, or wilfulness, or whatever.

OBJECTIONS

So far I have attempted to sketch an account of how the rationality of belief in a developed religion such as Christianity might be defended as a web, by a version of the coherentist approach to epistemic justification. Certain objections must now be considered.

First, the objection from unreality. Granted that the elements of the web cohere together, it may be that they are simply cohering in the way that the elements of a fairy story, or of a novel, cohere. A novel may hold together as a narrative, and even contain historical facts, and yet be overall fictitious. There's a sense in which one is defenceless against this type of criticism, and a sense in which one is not. There is no knockdown response to it. Nevertheless, given that (as has been argued) the web of religious belief is held within a wider set of empirical beliefs which may, for all we know, be justified differently, such extra-web beliefs may mitigate the force of the objection in two ways: by stressing the part played in supporting the web by general empirical or moral or metaphysical beliefs, and by personal experience. But the danger of vicious circularity remains, in that the integrative, central explanation may seem to explain the data best but only because it interprets or reinterprets the beliefs in doing so. The best answer to this objection is the adoption of a methodological principle of testing and retesting the relevant beliefs. Such testing is not the use of one kind of test, a linear test of the putative deductive or inductive links to the foundations; there is a variety of tests, testing how the proposition coheres with several different types of other beliefs in the web of belief, and how it relates to beliefs about matters outside the web.

The idea of Christian belief as an intricate web emphasizes the systematic, self-supporting character of such belief. But there is another aspect to this idea. To change the metaphor somewhat, this web reaches out; some of the propositions which form the web are, in virtue of their meaning, self-involving. This is not quite the point about self-involvement in Donald Evans's sense;[6] I don't involve *myself*, but belief in the web involves me, my experience, and expectations in the way in which a handbook for a car may contain information not only about the car, about how to modify it and maintain it, but also about how to get the maximum enjoyment and satisfaction from it. The web contains not only propositions but promises; not only threads but handholds and footholds.

So by 'coherence' is meant not only the logical consistency of the various propositions of the Christian faith, and the intelligibility that each part conveys to the whole, but also the power that set of propositions may have to explain the experience and history of any person who embraces it, to convey self-awareness and self-understanding. For one of the distinctive claims of Christianity is that it changes the life of any person who responds appropriately to its teaching. We must not rule out such claims by adopting a dogmatically a priori approach to the examination of its reasonableness. That would violate the James Principle. So the coherence in question is not merely that possessed by a narrative, but one that may involve the reader of the narrative, as reading a novel may change the self-understanding of the reader, say. The person-relative character of the coherence is evident again. More will be said about this in the next section.

[6] Donald M. Evans, *The Logic of Self-involvement* (London, 1963).

However, such appeals to coherence are not an effort to claim that the Christian faith is true *just because* it coheres with a person's experience. A distinction must be made between using coherence to account for the truth of Christianity, and using it to establish its truth, to promote belief in it. What makes the Christian faith true, if it is true, is that it is the case, it corresponds to the facts. But the fact that it corresponds to the facts cannot of itself serve to convince anyone of its truth, or of the reasonableness of believing that it is true. To do that there must be some kind of 'engagement' between the truth claims of the faith and the powers and interests and needs of the human person. And part of that engagement, I am suggesting, is the coherence of the Christian faith as such, and its connection with beliefs outside the web, and its relevance to some of the characteristic hopes, fears, and needs of a human being.

But in appealing to coherence in this way, to explanatory and personal fit, am I not, in effect, appealing to ineffability, claiming that God must be experienced, but that he cannot be thought about? Not at all. Sometimes, as we saw in the first chapter, the contrast is drawn between the personal and the propositional, and it is claimed that the relation between God and his rational creatures is a personal, non-propositional relationship. But nothing that I have said about the web of belief requires one to subscribe to such a view. For much of what a person experiences when the web of belief coheres with his needs and goals is capable of being expressed in propositional form. No person can do this exhaustively. Yet the web of the Christian faith, expressed in propositions which can be thought about, discussed, and argued over, is best established by its own power to present itself in a commanding, cohering manner in human experience. Once again, the content of the Christian faith must be distinguished from the manner in which that faith is presented for reasonable belief.

The reference to 'needs' may cause an eyebrow or two to rise. 'Are you saying that one reason for taking the Christian faith to be true is because it meets my needs?' Partly, yes—in the same way that it is a good reason to believe that what I have eaten is a piece of bread because it is nourishing me. The fact that it is nourishing me does not make it bread, but if it did not nourish me then it would not be bread. One of the claims made by the Christian faith is that its true reception results in the nourishing of the human spirit; it is therefore a reasonable ground for believing that the Christian faith is true that it nourishes those to whom it is presented and by whom it is received; that, in the broadest sense, it coheres with a person's experience even though it may involve some redescription of that experience. Such a defence of the rationality of a web of belief is not merely pragmatic or instrumental. It is rather the reverse. The claim is that a web of belief has instrumental value because of the meaning of its constituent propositions and their coherence, and the recognition and enjoyment of such value is a good criterion of its truth, though not of course the only criterion.

A further objection to the claims which I have been making about the web of belief is that this evidence provided by personal experience, by personal engagement, is the evidence of one person and so it is not to be relied upon. For may that person not be mistaken in the interpretation he gives of his experience? Earlier I mentioned memory beliefs. Memory is personal, indeed remembering is a person-relative activity *par excellence*. But the claims of memory can often be supported by other lines of enquiry, by presently experienced historical traces such as diaries and other historical documents, and by the present memory claims of other people.

To what propositions could an appeal be made showing that, given that set, it is reasonable to suppose that the Christian faith is true? Are there other true faiths to which we might refer for this purpose in order that from them we might make a generalization to the Christian faith? Clearly not. And not only clearly not, but necessarily not, at least not if the exclusive claims made by the Christian faith are to be taken at face value. Besides, the appeal to the reasonableness of the Christian faith based upon induction from analogous cases is quite out of keeping with the temper of Christianity, which presents itself as an astonishing, staggering thing, not as the sort of thing that is believable as a result of some inductive generalization.

I have tried to outline what I have called a reasonableness strategy by treating the cognitive side of the Christian faith as a web of belief. The aim of this strategy is not to buttress or support such a faith from outside itself, by introducing reasons additional to those provided by the faith itself, but by allowing those reasons to speak for themselves. In some cases this will involve philosophical issues and in other cases matters of fact. And one positive argument for the reasonableness of the Christian faith is that, taken as a whole, it is consistent with the experience of the one who accepts it, and illuminates that experience by, for example, providing an explanation of it, and redirecting it.

One implication of this argument is that there is no knockdown proof of the rationality of the Christian faith, a proof that will appeal to any rational man simply by virtue of his rationality, and correspondingly no knockdown proof of its irrationality. In this respect the epistemological position regarding belief in the Christian faith is one of parity with other faiths and ideologies. This will, to some, seem a very unsatisfactory position, because it may appear to demote their faith from a position of superiority over all other faiths to one in which, from a logical and dialectical point of view, it is exactly equivalent to any other religious or ideological position of comparable scope or coherence.

But there is no alternative to this view. The Christian faith is, from a formal epistemological point of view, exactly on a par with other religions, and of course they are on a par with it. This is not because there is a knockdown proof of the faith which believers in other faiths do not see the soundness of; it is because this is how the position must be under present circumstances.

So the reasonableness of the Christian faith does not lie in the fact that it provides a proof of its own truth which would be acceptable to any rational person. It is a gospel, a message of good news. The aim of any reasonableness strategy should be to allow that message to be heard unfettered and uncluttered by the baggage of intellectual misconception. Such parity in reasonableness between Christianity and other religions and ideologies, with each religion being reasonable to the minds of many of its adherents, does not mean that there is no such thing as objective truth. There is nothing incoherent or unacceptable in the view that a set of propositions is objectively true but that no formal proof of this objective truth can be provided. Is not this how it is with most objective truths about matters of fact?

THE WEB OF BELIEF AND THE NATURE OF FAITH

What consequences does the idea of a faith such as Christianity forming a web of propositions, and the reasonableness of that faith being supported by way of a web-like explanation, have for the nature of faith? It is often thought to be an essential feature of religious faith that it is certain. Earlier we noted Anthony Kenny's view, following Aquinas, that faith is belief in something as revealed by God, an attitude of certainty involving a commitment without reserve to the articles of faith. More recently in his book *Faith and Criticism*,[7] Basil Mitchell has made a similar point about the unreserved character of faith, in the face of the criticisms of D. Z. Phillips, maintaining the idea that faith is not tentative or hypothetical in character.

It seems to me that the issue of whether faith is, or is not, certain is based upon too monochrome a view of the evidential grounds of the belief component of faith. These grounds differ from proposition to proposition and from time to time. And is it not harsh to suppose that any attitude short of certainty could not form the doxastic component of faith? A person may hold some of the propositions of his faith with certainty, while other propositions may be held tentatively, with reservation, in just the same way that he may believe some things about the Battle of Waterloo (or the nature of cow's milk) with certainty, other things more tentatively. The belief in such cases of tentative faith may be more like the acceptance of an hypothesis than a firm belief in the truth of a proposition. There is no good reason to suppose, on the view of the propositions of faith as a web, that each proposition of the web is supported by the same degree of evidence,[8] as Kenny supposes that all the propositions of faith are backed by the same authoritative testimony, and are therefore to be believed with exactly the same degree of strength, or with at least the strength of certainty.

Mitchell's claim seems to be that there can be unconditional trust that p where p is nevertheless only subjectively probable or tentative. Granted, one could have unconditional trust in p when there is only a theoretical possibility that not-p. But it is harder to see how unconditionality can be sustained, or ought to be sustained, where there is some real epistemic probability that not-p.

Mitchell supports his position with the following example:

Let us imagine a backwoodsman living in a remote part of Quebec, who believes himself to owe unconditional obedience to the King of France. He does not realize that there has not been a King of France for over a century.

---

[7] Basil Mitchell, *Faith and Criticism* (Oxford, 1994).

[8] There is no a priori reason why there must be less evidence for a peripheral proposition than for a central or intermediate proposition. But it would be bizarre to suppose that there could be equal evidence for each proposition in the web, since some propositions provide evidence for the truth of others.

One day he comes into town and learns for the first time that there is no King of France and there has not been one during his lifetime. His unconditional obedience to the King of France presupposes that there is a King of France and is not to be construed as entailing an unconditional duty to go on believing that there is a King of France in the face of clear evidence to the contrary.[9]

He argues that this is a case of unconditional trust even where the object of trust, unbeknown to the one who trusts, no longer exists. But this is not quite to the point, which is: Can a person have unconditional trust that *p* in a situation where he believes that there is a real possibility (and not merely a theoretical possibility) that not-*p*? Not only can one trust in what does not exist, but since the relation between being psychologically certain and having correct beliefs is in any case a contingent one, one may feel confident that *p* where one's grounds for believing that *p* are nevertheless weak. But these points are not relevant here. The question here is not what can happen, but what ought to happen, and the confidence ought surely to have some positive relation to the evidence for the belief, not be unrelated to it.

A further difficulty with the example given by Mitchell is that the existence of God is not parallel with the case cited. In a cultural situation in which there is widespread disbelief as well as a plurality of faiths this fact is invariably transmitted to the cognitive apparatus of the believer, however ardent a believer he may be. (If the backwoodsman hears rumours of a French republic before he comes into town ought not his trust in the King of France to be immediately weakened?)

Further, a cumulative case strategy such as Mitchell's would appear to entail a conditional account of faith, or at least a conditional view of the evidence for some of the propositions of faith. So it is not easy to see how the doxastic aspect of faith can have a conditional character while the fiducial reliance that is characteristic of religious faith can be unconditional, if faith involves belief in some propositions which are peripheral to the web and therefore backed by a lower degree of evidence than the more central propositions. The fiducial commitment should surely be correlated with the degree of evidence supporting the proposition.

So I am arguing that the idea of the propositions of the faith form-

---

[9]   Mitchell, *Faith and Criticism*, 66.

ing a web is compatible with the proportionality view of religious faith outlined earlier, and that this is a more realistic and reasonable view than either Kenny's or Mitchell's. Whether it is more realistic than what in the first chapter I referred to as the 'evidential deficiency' view of faith is something we shall consider later on.

4

Accumulated Evidence

We have been examining the logical and epistemological structure of the claim that the justification of religious belief is a matter of the coherence of a web of belief. One prominent defender of such a strategy is Basil Mitchell, who in a number of writings, particularly *The Justification of Religious Belief*[1] and *Faith and Criticism*,[2] has (consciously or otherwise) followed the lead of Joseph Butler, who in the Introduction to *The Analogy of Religion* appeals to what he calls 'accumulated evidence'.[3]

In this chapter we shall give further consideration to the idea of accumulation or coherence by examining Mitchell's approach as a defence of the rationality of religion, rather than the rationality of religious belief, for that is what I think it is, despite the title of one of Mitchell's books. I take it that 'religion' is a somewhat wider term than, say, 'religious belief' or 'theistic belief'; for while it embraces such beliefs, or may do so, it also has other concerns: ethical and spiritual needs and goals and ideals, the relation of an individual to a tradition, and the fact and importance of corporate life. Religion is an orientation of oneself that includes all these, or may include them, and no doubt may include much else besides. When we are addressing the rationality of religion, therefore, considerations are relevant which are not relevant in the case of theistic belief alone, or even of religious belief. And the considerations relevant to the rationality of adherence to a religion may be as many-sided as religion itself. This is not only true of religion. A person's reasons for pursuing a career in science will be different from the reasons he may have for believing some proposition in science.

---

[1] Basil Mitchell, *The Justification of Religious Belief* (London, 1973).
[2] Basil Mitchell, *Faith and Criticism* (Oxford, 1994).
[3] Joseph Butler, *The Analogy of Religion*, in *Works*, ed. W. E. Gladstone (Oxford, 1897), i. 10.

Earlier I argued that 'rationality' is also a wideish notion, certainly wider and vaguer than the idea of epistemic justification, difficult though that notion itself is, though I suspect that Mitchell is using the two terms fairly interchangeably in his *The Justification of Religious Belief*, for example. For one thing, one can apply rationality not only to belief, but also to action. For another, the rationality of a belief or an action depends or may depend crucially on what one already believes about what is the case or what ought to be the case. So what it is rational for *A* to believe or to do might not be the same as what it is rational for *B* to believe or do. In the jargon, rationality is person-relative, a phrase that I want to look at more closely soon. So what follows is a contribution to rationality and religion, and to the rationality of religion, in these wideish senses.

At least part of Mitchell's intended programme is to defend the rationality of religious belief in the sense that involves theistic belief, and which focuses attention upon such belief in a situation in which it is highly disputed. That is, he wishes to defend the possibility of disputing about such fundamental matters rationally, and to sketch a way in which such differences might, in principle at least, be settled. And I hope that I am interpreting him correctly if I say that a necessary condition for calling any dispute between two or more people, including any religious dispute, a rational dispute is that such a dispute is one which endeavours to make the best sense of all the available evidence and which is capable, at least in principle, of being resolved by rational means.

While no doubt it is part of rationality to attempt to make the best sense of all the available evidence, in this chapter I want to take up Mitchell's phrase, 'settlable in principle by rational means', and to argue that in so far as the phrase can be given a clear meaning it is *not* a necessary condition for conflicting beliefs being rationally held that the differences be settlable in principle by rational means, and also to argue that this is particularly so in the case of religious belief, because of the presence and importance of person-relative beliefs in religion, and of the nature of religion itself. This argument, if it is successful, does not weaken the cumulative-case type of argument, but it does reduce its apologetic power.

In the first section of the chapter I shall discuss the idea of something being resolvable in principle by rational means, particularly as Basil Mitchell understands this. Then in the second section of the chapter I shall offer two reasons, or two types of reason, why even if we can be clear on what it means to resolve something in principle by rational means, there are certain kinds of dispute, among them certain kinds of religious dispute, or dispute over religion, that cannot be settled in principle, but that the religious (and of course irreligious) beliefs held in such disputes may nevertheless be rationally held.

RESOLVING DISPUTES BY RATIONAL MEANS

What is it to hold that a dispute is resolvable in principle by rational means? Presumably something like this: that there is a set of rational procedures which *A* and *B*, who are in disagreement about some fundamental matter, agree to be rational. And there is a set of conditions in which *A* and *B* agree about the truth of the disputed matter or the rationality of believing in the truth of what was previously disputed, as a result of using these procedures. Moreover, to get from the starting point to the finishing point, every step must be an application by *A* and *B* of such agreed rational procedures; or at least, every step in which considerations of rationality are relevant must be an application of such rational procedures for *A* and *B*. The importance Mitchell attaches to the idea of agreement in principle, even when there is no agreement in fact, is intended to preserve both the objectivity of the dispute, and the fact that each of the participants may claim to be rational in the absence of agreement, so long as each is striving to make the best sense of the available evidence, striving to be rational.

Mitchell takes certain kinds of basic scientific dispute as an important analogy for the religious case. He argues that some facts are theory- or presupposition-independent[4] and are agreed across theories, and he rejects Thomas Kuhn's claim that rational debate is either an exercise in strict logic, or else a matter of sociology or psychology.[5] It is a distortion to argue that if a difference cannot be settled by considerations of logical validity the difference must be a matter of psychology. There is a third alternative, that 'rational choice is possible between presuppositions, for they can be judged by their capacity to make sense of all the relevant evidence'.[6] So

---

[4] Mitchell, *The Justification of Religious Belief*, 79.   [5] Ibid. 83.
[6] Ibid. 91.

Mitchell sees a way to deny the claim that a rational solution to a disagreement is only ever possible where no profound conceptual differences are involved.[7]

According to Mitchell what is characteristic of rational dispute between the holders of rival metaphysical systems, including disputes of a religious kind, is that agreement is in principle possible, but that one cannot specify in advance the rational procedures by which such agreement in principle might be reached. These procedures therefore certainly cannot be, or cannot wholly be, inductive or demonstrative. The two points are obviously connected. If one could specify in advance what the rational procedures are, then one would be able to specify in advance the conditions for rational agreement. So on Mitchell's account, despite what I suggested earlier about what it means to resolve a dispute by rational means, two people *can* engage rationally in a dispute without knowing that they are doing so rationally, except in the general sense that each is striving to make the best sense of the evidence. Only after having made the best sense of it are they in a position to say how that feat was accomplished, but this will not be by describing the rules that they have followed, because they haven't been following any rules. If one is rational in circumstances of a deep religious dispute, then necessarily one does not know that one is in advance of the settling of the dispute.

So one interesting consequence of Mitchell's account of rational argument in religion, a consequence of the centrality and peculiar nature of the notion of *judgement* in his account, is that neither participant need be aware of the various procedures that they are employing in attempting to make the best sense of the evidence, and perhaps neither can be aware of them in advance, and so one may be carrying out rational procedures without being aware that one is. There are certain kinds of dispute which, if they are solved by the use of rational procedures, this fact is only apparent with hindsight. Such disputes are rational in that they are concerned with making sense of all the relevant evidence, but the procedures for making sense of the evidence cannot be specified, or specified fully, in advance.

I am not at all sure what Mitchell's argument is that leads to the conclusion that the Kuhnian objection, the objection that there can only be rational choice where the choosing is in accordance with the rules of deductive and inductive logic, is to be dismissed.[8] He later

[7] Ibid. 62.   [8] Ibid. 84–5.

says that 'to decide between these possibilities requires thought. If this exercise of thought has itself to be rule governed, the question can in turn be raised whether these rules have been correctly specified, and so on ad infinitum.'[9]

Why is this infinite regress inevitable? Why cannot the rules be specified in a regress-preventing way? One can specify the rules of inductive or deductive reasoning, or of football or chess, without facing an infinite regress, so why not in this case? And it looks mysterious to have a third way of reasoning besides deductive and inductive reasoning, a way which consists in making judgements each of which is *sui generis*. Such a claim faces an opposite criticism to the criticism that it involves an infinite regress: namely, that if each case of judgement is *sui generis*, how come each is none the less a rational procedure? One cannot, I think, reply that the *sui generis* procedure is rational simply because it aims to make the best sense of the total evidence, since presumably there may be non-rational procedures that also do this. A tea-leaf gazer may be striving to make the best sense of the total evidence.

How different is Mitchell's appeal to judgement from an appeal to intuition? Presumably the difference lies in the fact that after the exercise of judgement it is possible to convey to others how one reached the conclusion that one did in this particular case—though the procedures unwittingly followed in this particular case carry no precedent for other cases. The idea of procedures that one cannot specify in advance, and the consequent prominence given to the rather mysterious faculty of judgement, seem to me to be weaknesses in Mitchell's account.

I do not doubt that there are situations in which there are incommensurable factors and in which, if a decision has to be made, a decision to act, or if an interpretation of some complex historical or literary situation is attempted, an element of judgement is invariably required. Historical and literary debates of the sort that Mitchell has highlighted seem often to be cases of this, because each involves a matrix of many incommensurable factors; and certain kinds of moral dilemma are similar. It may also be that the question of whether adherence to a particular religion is rational or not is such a case. But before concluding that it is I want to explore an alternative possibility.

[9] Ibid. 89.

I argued in the previous chapter for a close connection between the idea of coherentist justification and the recognition that certain beliefs are what are called person-relative beliefs; roughly, beliefs which depend for their credibility upon matters which are not immediately available to anyone, and which may be available only to one person. This connection between the two may not, however, be a logical one. For the beliefs that one appeals to in order to display the coherence of one's case may all be general beliefs, beliefs not relative to particular persons, beliefs which all people share or may fairly easily share, beliefs which do not depend upon the fact that the one who holds them is Jones and not Smith. But I think that in the case of Basil Mitchell's procedure there *is* a logical connection between that hypothesis and the fact of person-relative belief, for a particular understanding of the availability of evidence is essential to his account of that hypothesis and of the operation of personal judgement in it. That is, there may be two individuals who each have available to them the same general evidence for a given hypothesis, but one may judge that the evidence tends to support that hypothesis, the other not. It is surely unsatisfactory to account for such divergence by anything that is purely subjective, or by an appeal to this rather mysterious faculty of judgement. Such a divergence is better explained, perhaps is only explicable, on the grounds that the credibility for each person of the general evidence for the hypothesis varies in the light of what each separately and already believes, their person-relative beliefs. It is in the light of what each separately believes that each makes his or her judgement.

So I have doubts about the idea of a fundamental religious dispute being resolvable by rational means in the manner proposed by Basil Mitchell. The idea of a procedure being rational yet of disputants not being able to settle the rules in advance; the place of judgement in the Mitchellian sense—these are to my mind obscure ideas. In the remainder of the chapter I shall offer two reasons, or two sorts of reason, for thinking that the claim that an issue can be settled in principle by rational means is *not* a necessary condition for the conflicting beliefs being rationally held, and I shall argue that this is particularly so in the case of religious belief.

THE PERSON-RELATIVITY OF RELIGIOUS BELIEF

One expression Mitchell repeatedly uses in his version of the cumulative case hypothesis is 'the availability of evidence': the rationality
and hence the objectivity of our procedures are secure so long as we
are trying to make sense of all the available evidence.

I shall argue that in the case of those religious beliefs which contain person-relative elements (and as I have argued it would appear
that Mitchell makes essential use of such beliefs in his account of the
accumulation of evidence), the presence of such beliefs is sufficient
for removing the obligation to seek the rational resolution of disputes as part of establishing the rationality of religious belief. For the
available evidence might be so distributed that it might be rational
for one person at time $t1$ and at all subsequent times to believe that
p, and rational for another person at time $t1$ and all subsequent times
to believe that not-p. (For ease of exposition we shall not concern
ourselves with degrees of belief, though these are clearly relevant.)

But what, more precisely, are person-relative beliefs? Or what is
the person-relative evidence that renders a proposition more probable to one person than to another? The existence of such beliefs does
not just signal the fact that evidence for beliefs is not total evidence,
or the evidence available to everyone, or the evidence available to an
impartial and ideal observer, for the recognition of such constraints
upon the availability of evidence is among the commonplaces of epistemology. No human belief is ever founded upon total evidence, and
if in the interests of rationality we restrict our beliefs to those for
which there is as a matter of fact evidence equally available to everyone, or to beliefs which in fact pass some general evidential thresh-
old, then we shall end up with very few rational beliefs indeed. In the
matter of beliefs and their justification, one must take account of the
fact that one is neither infallible nor omniscient.

Rather, person-relative evidence is evidence which as a matter of
fact a person possesses which another person could in principle have,
but cannot now obtain, or cannot now obtain very easily. For example, part of a person's evidence may be certain memories. Even if the
memories are of some public event, no person can now have that evidence who did not witness that event. But if the event recurs, as the
event of the appearance of a comet may recur, then other people can

have that evidence, or something very like that evidence, and come to share the beliefs of the first person, beliefs for example about the appearing and the appearance of the comet. If the memories are of some private happening, or of an event that will not recur, then the evidence is less accessible to other people. In so far as such person-relative beliefs may affect the reasonableness of a person believing other things, the influence of person-relative beliefs may spread throughout much of a person's noetic structure.

So a person-relative belief may simply be a belief that one person has better evidence for than another. For example, I believed five minutes ago that I had five coins in my pocket, and the evidence for this is that I touched them. You can now have the belief that Helm had five coins in his pocket five minutes ago if I tell you I did and you credit what I tell you, though your evidence for that belief is weaker than mine, if only because I might forget something in what I tell you, or unintentionally misdescribe the situation. But it is the same belief. Some beliefs which at first glance are beliefs which one person alone can have are not so once we get issues of indexicality straightened out, and perhaps the distinction between belief types and belief tokens.

But not only does each of us necessarily have less than total evidence for the truth of a belief; for at least some of our beliefs, perhaps for very many of them, even for most of them, we have unique evidence, evidence which as a matter of contingent fact has come to us, and as a matter of contingent fact has not come to others. Moreover this evidence in this strength cannot now be given to others; repeated reports of such evidence weaken its strength and therefore its convincingness; there is a principle of dilution at work due to a general belief in the fallibility and possible gullibility of the witness. This is why evidence that A has through direct experience cannot be conveyed with the same strength to B, and from B to C and so on.

I don't mean that the principle of dilution works always and only one way. I'm not arguing, in other words, that beliefs acquired directly and not as the result of the testimony of others are always stronger than their reported versions. Sometimes we need to correct our personally acquired beliefs by other beliefs that we have, and by beliefs that others communicate to us. Nevertheless, I think that the truth behind the epistemological significance of the idea of person-relative beliefs is that of the epistemic privilege of certain of our beliefs, a privilege which confers an epistemic advantage, though one that is defeasible.

Another factor accounting for the significance of person-relative beliefs is the necessary under-description of our direct experience. Our direct experience is often if not always richer and more manifold than are the words we use to represent it to ourselves and to others. Philosophers set great store by words, and properly so, but it is a commonplace that words cannot convey the feltness and immediacy of experience, nor the vividness and complexity of the beliefs that immediately arise upon that experience. In saying this, I am not appealing to ineffability, nor am I arguing that verbalizing our experience necessarily distorts it, but I am simply drawing attention to our human limits of articulation. So here is another sense in which we might talk of person-relative beliefs, complex beliefs that supervene on the incommunicable feltness and immediacy of an experience.

For clarity, let us distinguish between eliminable and ineliminable person-relative beliefs. An example of an eliminable person-relative belief would be the following. Suppose that it is reasonable for me to believe that I have five coins in my pocket by remembering that I put them there. Because your epistemic situation is different from mine, it may be less reasonable for you to believe it. But I might make it more reasonable for you to believe this, and even as reasonable for you to believe it as it is for me to believe it, by showing you the coins and then replacing them in my pocket. I have then eliminated our differences.

Whatever the details, it is clear that there are some person-relative beliefs which are eliminable; you and I can each come to believe the same proposition with the same degree of evidence. But are all person-relative beliefs eliminable? In his discussion of the justification of religious belief Mitchell, having cited cases of literary and historical disagreement and agreement, extends these, through a consideration of issues from the philosophy of science, to disputes in which fundamental conceptual differences are involved. He offers cases of disputes of this kind, but which are capable, 'at least in principle, of being resolved by rational means'.[10] I think that resolution in principle is true in the case of disputes which involve only eliminable person-relative beliefs, but not of disputes which involve ineliminable person-relative beliefs, and such beliefs, I claim, are characteristic of one kind of argument for religion, namely that kind which appeals to immediate religious experience or awareness, and also to the more

---

[10] Mitchell, *The Justification of Religious Belief*, 74.

common cases where the evidence of direct memory is part of the evidence for religious belief.

So the relativity of certain person-relative beliefs is ineliminable. If in such cases we none the less wish to appeal to the availability of evidence in principle (as Mitchell does) then I suggest that we are stretching the idea of availability to breaking point. As we have seen, there is a familiar and straightforward sense in which one may make evidence available: by sharing data such as diaries and textbooks, by seeing things together under broadly similar conditions, and so on. But there are some types of evidence which you at present possess which, in order for that evidence to be made available to me, would require me to be you, or at least require me to have direct access to your mental states. And if such access is logically impossible, or logically impossible now, then there is no possible world in which such evidence is available, or is available now, and the Mitchellian phrase 'available in principle' is inapplicable to such cases.

There are also experiences which a person has had, and the beliefs that arise from these experiences, or which such experiences might confirm. Are these data available in principle? Is, say, Luther's sense of his deep dissatisfaction with himself available in principle to us? Is, say, Isaiah's vision in the Temple available in principle to us? If not, and if the sense of dissatisfaction, and the awareness conveyed by the vision, increased the rationality of some religious belief for Luther or for Isaiah (as we might suppose), then the rationality of religious belief for a person may be based upon, or may be increased by, the ineliminable person-relative beliefs of that person.

We could have an experience *like* Isaiah's, perhaps. But for it to have the evidential significance it had for Isaiah, we would have to experience it under conditions that, broadly speaking, Isaiah did. Is this possible? Even if we could be transported back in time to Isaiah's strange world, whether or not we could or would have had such an experience is not, presumably, up to us. For a consciously self-induced experience like Isaiah's would not be Isaiah's experience, not even a token of the same type. No doubt there is a possible world in which, say, Karl Marx and Isaiah hold the same religious opinions, having arrived at them rationally. To that extent the phrase 'agreement in principle' has a meaning. But such a world may be inaccessible from the actual world, the world in which Karl Marx and Isaiah deeply disagree. That is, it may be impossible to construct a finite set of steps involving rational procedures from present disagreement to future agreement.

So each of us is in a unique cognitive position, which may or may not be significant, depending upon what we actually cognize, or claim to. I cannot now return with you to what I experienced and which you (had you been present) could also have experienced. In addition, in the case of private experiences such as visions, dreams, or vivid memories, I am uniquely positioned in a stronger sense, that no one can bring it about, now or ever, that you have precisely these data, for to have them you would have to be me.

Mitchell's type of cumulative case argument admits of such ineliminable person-relative beliefs. He does not propose a method for eliminating person-relative beliefs, a method such as that of Descartes, say, or of Locke on some readings, but rather of endorsing such beliefs, indeed giving them centre stage in characterizing what it is for a religious belief, and certain other kinds of belief, to be rational. As he says,

There are many people who lack any form of religious sensitivity, who have never at any time worshipped, or prayed or felt at all tempted to worship or pray, whose response to religious music or religious architecture has always been purely aesthetic, who at no time have experienced any radical dissatisfaction with themselves and their accepted ends or any sense of impenetrable mystery. It is inevitable that such persons should be defective in their appreciation of theism.[11]

I take it that when Mitchell says that 'The individual scholar's moral, aesthetic or spiritual appreciation directly affects, in many cases, his capacity to understand what he is talking about and to make sound judgements about it'[12] this is another piece of evidence that Mitchell takes the factor of person-relativity seriously.

Perhaps we can generalize the point about the centrality of ineliminable person-relative beliefs in Mitchell's account of the justification of religious belief as follows. Anyone who, like Mitchell, takes seriously the idea of appealing to revelation (in a fairly traditional sense) as part of the cumulative case for religious belief must also take seriously the idea of ineliminable person-relative beliefs. In fact theories of revelation can be distinguished by whether or not they are committed to ineliminable person-relative beliefs. If, say, like the deists and like Kant, revelation is a republication of the truths or principles of reason, then the status of the revelation is unaffected by the elim-

---

[11] Mitchell, *The Justification of Religious Belief*, 103.   [12] Ibid.

ination of any person-relative beliefs it may report. They are part of the form and not the content of the revelation. But if revelation is a source of truths not otherwise available, then it is necessary that there are ineliminable person-relative beliefs as part of the revelation.

Person-relative beliefs ought not to be confused with purely subjective preferences or states. For they are consistent with what might be called the principle of the supervenience of belief upon evidence. That is, if it is reasonable for A on evidence E to believe that p then it would also be reasonable for B on evidence E to believe that p. The only problem is, B may not have such evidence for p and may never be able to obtain it. If, *per impossibile*, I had been Isaiah, or indistinguishable from Isaiah, then the experience in the Temple should have increased the rationality of my religious belief as (we are assuming) it did for Isaiah. Contrast subjectivism, where no such principle of supervenience applies. On a purely subjectivist view of belief formation a person may properly believe p when the evidence favours r, or alternatively when it favours neither p nor r. Of course a person may have a reason for such a belief, but it is not a reason grounded in or arising out of the evidence; perhaps it is whimsical or the fruit of wishful thinking. He may delude himself that he has evidence for p when he has nothing of the kind.

In the interests of achieving objectivity, or of coming to agreement, perhaps we should strive to eliminate as many such person-relative beliefs as we can, but it is hard to see how we could eliminate all of them, and hard to see what argument might be used to urge such total elimination on us. If we cannot eliminate them, and if for something to be a proof it has to convince most people, then the existence of ineliminable person-relative beliefs places severe restrictions upon what one person might convince someone else of. That is, while one may convince someone of the formal validity of an argument, one cannot similarly convince that person of the conclusion of the argument unless that person accepts the premises, or accepts the premises with the appropriate degree of strength.

So far I have said something about what person-relative beliefs are, and argued against their total eradicability, while maintaining that such beliefs are essential to a Mitchell-type cumulative case argument for the rationality of religious belief. In such a situation two people may apply the same standards of reasonableness and find it reasonable to believe different things because they have different epistemic starting points.

This is my first type of argument for the conclusion that differences over religion may still be rational though irresolvable.

THE NATURE OF RELIGION

The second type of argument is derived from the nature of religion.

In considering the idea of the rationality of religion at the beginning of the chapter I suggested that religion is a different notion from religious belief, just as religious belief is a different notion from theistic belief. I want to develop this point as part of my second argument against the idea that only if differences are rationally resolvable are the relevant beliefs rational. Perhaps at this stage we move to considering a different objective of rational enquiry from the one that Mitchell has in *The Justification of Religious Belief*, though I am not entirely convinced of this. For although 'religious belief' is in the title of Mitchell's book, in fact he seems to have something different in mind in the book itself.

What I shall argue is that different people may want different things from religion, and that the only way of adjudicating between many such wants is by considering whether religion, or a particular religion, is a possible, or likely, means to gaining these ends. Hence it is unacceptably stipulative to claim that the rationality of religion ought to turn wholly on evidential matters, even if the rationality of religious belief should, and even if some of this evidence is person-relative in the sense discussed.

I wish to introduce my second argument by considering an aspect of Alvin Plantinga's exposition of 'Reformed' epistemology. At first glance, Plantinga's exposition is a good example of a contribution to the debate about whether the rationality of religious belief is to be settled on evidential considerations. He holds, as we saw earlier, that there are beliefs, including religious beliefs, which one does not need evidence for, though one may have grounds for such beliefs. Grounds are not evidence for Plantinga, because they are conditions and circumstances relative to a person, experiences rather than beliefs, though it is hard to see how beliefs would not be formed on the basis of such experiences. Grounds have the effect of removing arbitrariness. However, it is just here, in the sort of thing that for Plantinga counts as a ground, that he seems to reveal that what he has in mind is not the rationality of religious belief, but the rationality of religion:

Upon reading the Bible, one may be impressed with a deep sense that God is speaking to him. Upon having done what I know is cheap, or wrong, or wicked, I may feel guilty in God's sight and form the belief that God disapproves of what I have done. Upon confession and repentance I may feel forgiven, forming the belief that God forgives me for what I have done. A person in grave danger may turn to God, asking for his protection and help; and of course he or she then has the belief that God is indeed able to hear and help if he sees fit. When life is sweet and satisfying, a spontaneous sense of gratitude may well up within the soul; someone in this condition may thank and praise the Lord for his goodness, and will of course have the accompanying belief that indeed the Lord is to be thanked and praised.[13]

These examples are interesting in several ways, but I particularly wish to focus on the considerations of personal danger that Plantinga introduces. He makes it plain that considerations of personal danger and deliverance are relevant in the grounding of religious belief, relevant in displaying its rationality. Religious belief is at least partly grounded in a religious sense, in the awareness of a religious need. But if so, then rationality in religion is not limited to the domain of the purely external evidential features of a person's situation. By this I mean that what grounds a religious belief, and so makes it a non-arbitrary belief, and a fit candidate (according to Reformed epistemology) for a place in the foundations of a person's noetic structure, includes matters which the person believes are relevant to his own well-being. In saying this I do not mean that questions of danger and deliverance (if we take this as a typical example) are not cognitive in character. Let us suppose that they are, though we could argue about that. Rather what I mean is that grounding one's belief in God on such matters as the removal of danger and the sense of being forgiven involves one in introducing considerations that are not only concerned with issues of one's situation that are evidential but also with one's own hopes and fears. It is only a person so concerned about his guilt and deliverance who will ground his belief in the way sketched by Plantinga, and obviously not all are so concerned. And as we have seen, on this point at least Mitchell agrees with Plantinga since he also appeals to matters which are not purely

---

[13] Alvin Plantinga, 'Reason and Belief in God', in Alvin Plantinga and Nicholas Wolterstorff (eds.), *Rationality and Religious Belief* (Notre Dame, Ind., 1983), 80.

evidential, such as a sense of dissatisfaction with oneself and a general religious sensitivity.[14]

So the sense of rationality here includes not only rationality about matters of fact about one's situation, and matters of fact about oneself, but means–end rationality, practical rationality. It is practically rational, for anyone who is concerned about his own forgiveness, to think that a religion which makes provision for forgiveness is more rationally acceptable than one that does not. For anyone who is concerned about the rationality of religious belief, or the rationality of belief in a particular religion such as Christianity, as opposed to the rationality of theistic belief more abstractly considered, this is surely a relevant consideration. For religion, and certainly the Christian religion, is concerned not only with purely evidential matters, but with matters which concern ideals, spiritual fulfilment, well-being, and the like. And whether or not it is rational to participate in that religion may partly turn on considerations that are wider than the purely evidential, without discounting these. Questions of truth are important; but they may not be all-important. So I am not arguing that one has to be reductionistic or even Kantian about the truth claims of a religion in order to accept the point that different people want different things from religion. A person may accept that her particular religion makes truth claims, and recognize that the worthwhileness of the goals or ideals of her religion arise from these truth claims, but nevertheless attach less importance to satisfying herself over the truth claims of her religion than to participating in its procedures for obtaining forgiveness, or for achieving some other goal. And she can be rational in so doing.

Of course questions about how we should act cannot determine questions of truth or falsity. The fact that the cognizer is also an agent, with a variety of interests, may affect the amount of time and effort he is prepared to put into cognizing, and I am arguing that decisions about such preparedness may be addressed with unimpeachable rationality. Nevertheless the sort of rationality required to assess evidence, theoretical rationality as it is sometimes called, is different from practical rationality.

So one may reckon that religion is primarily and indispensably cognitive and that the truth or falsity of its claims is to be discerned only by reference to evidential considerations, while nevertheless

---

[14] Mitchell, *The Justification of Religious Belief*, 103.

holding that other things besides investigating the evidential grounds of one's religion have a higher priority in one's overall rational plan. It may be rational to believe that *p*, even while not investigating the evidential basis of *p*, if what is believed informs or renders intelligible certain otherwise intractable religious goals and ideals. So there may be two people who have the same evidence for a belief, and the same standards of evidential enquiry, but one may regard it as important that he subject his belief to further investigation, while the other may be content with the present evidential grounding of the belief because the truth thus believed satisfies other ends for which the securing of additional evidence would not be relevant.

A person might approach religion in the following way: if you can prove to me that a particular religion is more probable than not then I'll take whatever that religion has to offer. But another may say, I want a religion that offers forgiveness, though only, of course, if there is evidence for its truth.

So the two sorts of belief that we have been at pains to distinguish, beliefs about the world outside the self and beliefs about one's own desires and needs, may happily cohere, but they may also come apart. A person may want what the God for whom he has reasonable grounds to believe in cannot give. And he may on that account cease to believe that God exists, or the belief that God exists may remain a merely theoretical belief. Alternatively, a person may want what only God can give but lack sufficient evidence to make belief in such a God a reasonable belief, and so may despair.

But not only may these two types of belief be out of harmony, it is possible to envisage a trade-off between the one type of belief and the other. One of the ways in which the question of the rationality of religious belief may be unsettlable, besides the fact that relevant evidence may not be generally available because of the person-relative nature of the belief, is the fact that different people may place different values on the importance of having well-grounded religious belief and on the ends of religion as they understand these. If, in a Martin Luther-like way, a person has an overriding personal concern to be rid of his guilt before God, then it may be rational for him to become an adherent of a religion that holds out the prospect of such deliverance even though the evidential grounds for that religion are weak. Or suppose that one was generally sceptical about the possibility of settling fundamental religious issues on purely evidential grounds; in that situation of evidential equilibrium, it might be rational for a person with an overriding concern to be rid of his guilt to subscribe to a religion which offered deliverance from guilt. One might, in this way, offer a defence of the rationality of religion which has some of the features of Pascal's Wager. Indeed, adapting Pascal, one may say that the heart may have reasons that evidence knows nothing about.

It may be thought that the fact that different people place different values upon religion, have different concepts of religion and what it is supposed to do—the role that religion is to play in life—is deplorable. But it seems to me to be a plain matter of fact, and if so it is surely a relevant fact in discussing the rationality of religion.

CONCLUSION

John Locke famously and eloquently argued that 'he that believes, without having any reason for believing may be in love with his own fancies; but neither seeks truth as he ought, nor pays obedience due to his Maker'.[15] It is the overall argument of this book that Locke is correct, and this book aims to provide one plausible understanding of what it is to have a reason for a belief, and especially belief in a developed religion such as Christianity. Part of this involves the idea of there being a cumulative case for the reasonableness of Christianity. But it is doubtful whether Mitchell's form of a cumulative case argument can satisfy Locke's requirement. For central to Mitchell's proposal is a rather opaque account of evidential judgement.

But I have also argued that when it comes to the rationality of religion, wider considerations than the purely evidential intrude, and that a person may take due notice of these, while not of course denying the importance of evidence for the rationality of religious belief, without necessarily leaving himself open to Locke's charge that he is in love with his own fancies. The accumulation that he undertakes will include evidence, but it need not exclude everything else, and perhaps must not exclude everything else.

I think that in *The Justification of Religious Belief* and elsewhere Basil Mitchell recognizes this. His book is not in fact about the justification of religious belief, but about the rationality of adherence to

---

[15] John Locke, *Essay Concerning Human Understanding*, iv. xvii. 24.

a religion. However, I think that, as I have argued, one can account for differences over such adherence in terms of differences in beliefs and desires, without invoking, as Mitchell characteristically does, the mysterious faculty of judgement.

5

Belief and Believing

In recent years a good deal of attention has been paid to the question of whether, in order for belief in God to be rational, it is necessary to have reasons for such belief. As we saw in Chapter 2, it has not only been argued that strong foundationalism is referentially incoherent, and weak foundationalism permissible, but it has also been claimed that a person is within his epistemic rights to take the proposition 'God exists' as part of the foundations of his noetic structure, even though it is not evident to just any rational person that God exists. Even though one may be able to prove that God exists by using steps that are self-evident, from premises that are self-evident, one need not do this in order for one's belief in God to be rational. It is sufficient that that belief be a properly grounded part of an individual person's basic noetic structure.

Precedent for this last claim, if not warrant for it, has been found in John Calvin. 'Reformed' epistemology takes encouragement from the fact that in Calvin one finds very little attention given to the proofs of God's existence in either the Thomist or the Enlightenment senses. There is little interest in developing a natural theology, and no requirement that a person ought to be able to prove that God exists, or to have that proof made by another on his behalf, in order for his belief in God's existence to be rational. Instead, in the early parts of the *Institutes* and elsewhere, one finds Calvin insisting on the fact that everyone has the knowledge of God. Everyone has the *sensus divinitatis*, the seed of religion. And so it is claimed that Calvin is a foundationalist, though not a strong foundationalist in the Enlightenment sense, nor even in the more modest sense of Thomas Aquinas, in which the Five Ways may be taken to be instances not of faith seeking an indispensable rational foundation for itself but of faith seeking understanding, and attaining, in its core theistic claims, to the level of *scientia*.

But is Calvin in fact a foundationalist? In 'Reason and Belief in

God'[1] Alvin Plantinga cites passages from the *Institutes* regarding the *sensus divinitatis*, including this one:

Lest anyone, then, be excluded from access to happiness, he not only sowed in men's minds that seed of religion of which we have spoken but revealed himself and daily discloses himself in the whole workmanship of the universe. As a consequence, men cannot open their eyes without being compelled to see him.[2]

And Plantinga then draws the following conclusion:

Calvin's claim is that one who accedes to this tendency and in these circumstances accepts the belief that God has created the world—perhaps upon beholding the starry heavens, or the splendid majesty of the mountains, or the intricate, highly articulate beauty of a tiny flower—is entirely within his epistemic rights in doing so. It is not that such a person is justified or rational in so believing by virtue of having an implicit argument— some version of the teleological argument, say. No; he does not need any argument for justification or rationality. His belief need not be based on any other propositions at all; under these conditions he is perfectly rational in accepting belief in God in the utter absence of any argument, deductive or inductive. Indeed, a person in these conditions, says Calvin, *knows* that God exists.[3]

Perhaps Plantinga's comments amount to this, that Calvin offers what is an enthymemetic argument from the premise that there are people who without argument have the belief that God exists to the conclusion that they are entitled to such a belief. The suppressed premise is something like

It is rational to believe in God's existence without argument.

But is this a reasonable conclusion to draw from Calvin? There is reason to think that it is not. For one thing, there is no evidence from the passages cited (or from any similar passages) that Calvin has in mind the rationality of religious belief, or the nature of religious knowledge. Plantinga also quotes remarks of Calvin about the fact that the authority of Scripture is based not on 'rational proofs' but that the conviction that the Bible is the word of God ought to rest 'in

[1] Alvin Plantinga, 'Reason and Belief in God', in Alvin Plantinga and Nicholas Wolterstorff (eds.), *Faith and Rationality* (Notre Dame, Ind., 1983).

[2] John Calvin, *Institutes of the Christian Religion*, trans. F. L. Battles (London, 1960), I. v. 1, pp. 51–2; quoted in Plantinga, 'Reason and Belief in God', 66.

[3] Plantinga, 'Reason and Belief in God', 67; italics his.

a higher place than human reasons, judgements, or conjectures, that is, in the secret testimony of the Spirit'.[4]

There is certainly a kind of proportion here between Calvin's remarks and the denial of strong foundationalism: according to Calvin, in the case of the knowledge of God men do not have reasons, while in the case of the authority of Scripture men do not *need* reasons; at least, no reasons that are to be found only outside the Bible itself. But there is also a significant lack of proportion, for in discussing the authority of the Bible Calvin is making a normative claim, a claim about where we *ought* to ground our conviction that the Bible is the word of God. But it is not at all clear that these remarks about the self-authenticating character of the Bible apply, in Calvin's mind, to belief in God's existence. Calvin's appeal to the *sensus divinitatis* appears to be a factual claim.

We find in Calvin, I suggest, little or no interest in the rationality of religious belief. (Rationality in this sense is perhaps as much a child of the Enlightenment as is strong foundationalism; certainly one struggles to find any interest in such an issue in Calvin.) Rather, what Calvin emphasizes is not rationality but responsibility. His interest in the knowledge of God which he claims that all men have is not an interest in the rational grounds for theistic belief, but in establishing that since all men and women have some knowledge of God, they are culpable when they do not form their lives in a way that is appropriate to such knowledge.

For how can the thought of God penetrate your mind without your realising immediately that, since you are his handiwork, you have been made over and bound to his command by right of creation, that you owe your life to him?— that whatever you undertake, whatever you do, ought to be ascribed to him?[5]

Since, therefore, men one and all perceive that there is a God and that he is their Maker, they are condemned by their own testimony because they have failed to honour him and to consecrate their lives to his will.[6]

So while it may be implausible to employ Calvin in the interests of furthering a debate about the rationality of religious belief, his words about the *sensus divinitatis* do provide a reason for raising an issue that is less frequently discussed in debates about the rationality of

---

[4] Ibid. 67. See also Paul Helm, 'John Calvin, the *Sensus Divinitatis*, and the Noetic Effects of Sin', *International Journal for the Philosophy of Religion*, 43 (1998), 87–107.
[5] Calvin, *Institutes*, I. ii. 2, p. 42.   [6] Ibid. I. iii. I, p. 44.

religious belief. This is the question of the noetic effects of a person's moral condition. For Calvin, standing in a broadly Augustinian tradition, appears to claim that a person's moral and spiritual condition has epistemological consequences; that people have theological and religious differences not simply because they have different kinds of evidence available to them and have differences in investigative capabilities, persistence, and intelligence, or because they benefit differently from the results of past investigation, but because of something which is more basic than that, a prior disposition. It is this idea that I wish to investigate in this chapter.

Earlier I argued that according to the view of religious faith that I am defending, faith requires beliefs of two sorts. The first sort is beliefs which depend upon evidence of what is true, and the second sort is beliefs about what the believer wants or needs, his goals and ideals. We have seen, in the previous chapter, how it is possible to give an account of rationally held differences in religion in terms of differences in person-relative beliefs, and also in terms of what different people want. In this chapter we shall explore some of the consequences of the fact that these two sorts of beliefs may be at odds with each other. A person may want what God cannot give, and so cease to believe that this God exists (though so desperate may he be to believe in something that he may believe in an idol). Alternatively a person may want what God, if he exists, can give, but lack evidence, or sufficient evidence, for his existence, and so despair.

ACCOUNTING FOR UNBELIEF

How is unbelief to be accounted for? Broadly speaking there are two views. One is the answer given by the person I shall call the natural evidentialist. Unbelief is due to ignorance: ignorance of the balance of probabilities (if one is an evidentialist of the kind exemplified by, say, John Locke or Richard Swinburne) or plain ignorance of relevant facts. An alternative evidentialist answer is to say that religious belief is due to credulity, to giving the evidence more credit than is strictly due to it. As we saw when discussing Basil Mitchell's proposals, a popular view is that religious differences are due not to differences over the facts but to differences over the interpretations of those facts. All believing involves judging. All seeing is seeing as, and faith is, or is like, seeing as. Just as one can selectively attend to this feature of one's environment or that, seeing the shape on the page as a duck or as a rabbit, so, it is said, the believer and the unbeliever inhabit a neutral, epistemically underdetermined environment which they variously interpret. One sees an event as pure luck, the other as the providential goodness of God. One sees a zealot crucified on a cross, the other sees the death of the young Prince of Glory; and so on.

The view that I argued for does not deny any of these factors, but adds another: the presence of the ineradicable person-relativity of belief, the fact that the stock of beliefs of one person differs from that of another partly because of who they are, their respective unique personal histories. But besides all these factors which offer accounts of belief and unbelief which centre around the notion of evidence and its appropriate interpretation, there may be another.

It should be obvious from the passages which I have quoted that Calvin takes a more jaundiced view of human nature than is strictly implied by the fact either of mere ignorance, or of seeing as, or of personal relativity. Unlike the seeing-as view, the differences between believer and unbeliever do not lie at the level of interpretation, but at the level of the facts. There is a fact of the matter the evidence for which, or some of the evidence for which, the believer has possession of, or some grasp of, which the unbeliever has no possession of, or less grasp of. Calvin by implication joins the evidentialist in denying the subjectivism which lurks around the edges of the seeing-as approach. And of course he is not alone in this.

On the other hand, unlike the evidentialist—but in this respect at least like those who stress the importance of seeing as—and in a way that is at least consistent with the idea of beliefs as person-relative, Calvin maintains that basic religious differences are not due simply to ratiocinative mistakes, to miscalculation or misperception of the facts, or different epistemic histories, but to prior moral dispositions which filter and distort the data. Put in terms of our earlier discussion, these moral dispositions are beliefs about what a person wants, what that person believes to be an ideal worth achieving. And Calvin claims that it is (partly at least) because of the presence of such beliefs that people who have them fail to recognize the hand of God.[7] It is this idea, that there are, as I shall put it, moral preconditions for

---

[7] This, I believe, is the key to why in bk. 1 of the *Institutes* Calvin links together the knowledge of God and of ourselves.

learning facts, that I wish to explore. In fact I wish to explore two related ideas: that as a matter of fact our moral bias may lead us to misinterpret matters of fact, including facts about ourselves, and to neglect evidence, particularly where our own interests are affected; and that there are moral facts that we may miss or misperceive due to the presence in us of moral bias or conditioning.

THE FACT OF BIAS

There can be little doubt that on the first point, the fact of bias, Calvin and whoever thinks like him on this matter are correct. Our biases do affect our assessment of the evidence. This is notoriously so in the case of evidence about ourselves which affects our self-worth, our reputation, or our comfort, and about those people and matters in which we have a close interest. As Thomas Hobbes trenchantly expressed it,

the doctrine of right and wrong, is perpetually disputed, both by the pen and the sword: whereas the doctrine of lines and figures, is not so; because men care not, in that subject, what be truth, as a thing that crosses no man's ambition, profit or lust. For I doubt not, but if it had been a thing contrary to any man's right of dominion, or to the interests of men that have dominion, *that the three angles of a triangle, should be equal to two angles of a square*; that doctrine should have been, if not disputed, yet by the burning of all books of geometry, suppressed, as far as he whom it concerned was able.[8]

Like Hobbes, then, John Calvin draws attention to the connection between belief and value or interest, in terms of the characteristically modern ideas of suppression and projection; because belief in God *matters*, people take pains to fashion a comfortable God with whom to cohabit, or find atheism a more attractive prospect. Atheists may point to the solace of faith; but there may be no less solace in unbelief. The question is not whether suppression and projection happen, because of course they do happen. Suppression and projection happen in many areas of life but especially, as Calvin was quick to point out, in religion, where men and women project their own values and

---

[8] Quoted in Merold Westphal, 'Taking St. Paul Seriously: Sin as an Epistemological Category', in Thomas P. Flint (ed.), *Christian Philosophy* (Notre Dame, Ind., 1990), 204–5.

ideals onto God or onto something other than God. So in what follows I wish to argue that it is an implication of the argument that Calvin employs that not only religious believers may project and suppress; unbelievers may also do the same.

There can be no doubt that moral bias—or, to be less prejudicial, moral influence—does affect the character of what we claim to know, and of what we believe. The interesting question is whether the only responsibility that we have in this area, the only intellectual responsibility, is a purely negative one—to try as far as possible to stop the influence of such bias. Granted that we are afflicted by bias, bias which may prevent us forming a true estimate of ourselves, or a true estimate of what are authentic human values and ideals, is it our duty as far as possible to eliminate it, to hone our intellectual equipment, and to take possession of as many relevant facts as we can? Well, obviously it is important to be free of bias. Everyone is against sin. The more difficult question, and the question that Calvin and the Augustinian (and Pauline) tradition challenge us about is, What is bias?

Is there not only, as we have noted, bias which subverts evidence, and also moral bias, but also moral bias which subverts evidence? This is the second half of our question, and the more controversial. So what I wish to *explore*—and I stress that word—in the remainder of this chapter is the connection between interest and the appreciation of evidence. I will argue that there is a real possibility that there is such bias.

Let us recall the person that we earlier called the natural evidentialist, someone who believes that the question of whether religious belief is rational can only be settled on evidence assessed by reason—deductive and inductive—and by the senses. John Locke is a good example of such a natural evidentialist about religious belief. Such a person might believe that among the relevant evidence are issues of morality; but then, if a natural evidentialist is consistent at this point, he would hold a naturalistic meta-ethic.

By contrast, it is possible, given an objectivist meta-ethic of a non-natural kind, to hold what one might call non-natural evidentialism. This is evidentialism, for evidence and only evidence is relevant to settling issues of religious belief, but it also maintains that the evidence can be appreciated only in a way appropriate to the kind of fact in question. Non-moral facts are appreciated by our senses, while the truth of moral matters can only be assessed by what I shall call, deliberately vaguely, our moral nature. There may be evidence for moral facts which enters into the characterization of what a person adopts or retains as his goals and ideals, which a person with a certain sort of moral disposition will miss, or misinterpret. By this phrase 'moral nature', or 'moral disposition', I mean that assemblage of interests and abilities which concern the appreciation of moral matters. Whether or not this assemblage also constitutes a nature in some more precise sense is a question that I shall not attempt to investigate. Calvin is such a non-natural evidentialist; or that, at least, is how I shall interpret his words in this chapter. According to him, because of bias there are facts which the natural evidentialist will miss; but also—and more significantly for us—there are facts which a non-natural evidentialist will miss if he is biased in a certain way. Appeal to bias does not signal a retreat to subjectivism or non-cognitivism.

As a case of this, take someone who has a moral block, as when one has an obligation that one fails to recognize, like King David as revealed in the story of Nathan's parable. Here it is plausible to suppose that the situation is to be explained by there being a moral fact of the matter that a person, for whatever reason, fails to discern. Through the operation of bias a person may fail to see the objective wrongness of his action, just as due to a false sense of guilt or an exaggerated sense of fallibility a person may fail to see that what he did was, objectively speaking, the right thing to do.

One theme which—I hope you have noticed—runs throughout the previous chapters is that faith, certainly Christian faith, has not only a natural-evidential dimension, the dimension captured by the belief component of faith, but also a moral-evidential component. It is rational to trust another person, including God, only if that person is judged to be worth trusting; and that judgement may involve a judgement not only about the evidence supporting the belief that God, or a God of a certain sort, exists, but also a judgement about the moral character of the putative object of trust. It is because the object of faith, God himself, is reckoned to have a moral character, and is believed to have said or done things which are morally significant, and which affect the deepest interests of everyone, that beyond the question of belief the question of faith arises.

The distinction between natural evidence and moral evidence which I am attempting to draw is not between objective evidence and subjective interests, but between two different kinds of evidence for two different kinds of objective states of affairs. Our moral or passional natures (to use William James's phrase) may be vehicles for assessing part of the total evidence for the truth of a proposition, part of which may be empirical evidence, part of which may be evidence available only to our moral sense, or which may be available to us only if our moral sense is functioning in appropriate ways. And perhaps the difference between faith and unbelief is sometimes to be accounted for by a difference in the appreciation of moral evidence, or by differences in the values which people adhere to. If this is so, it would be natural that where there is disagreement each party should portray the other as projecting their values onto the evidence that there is for certain matters of fact.

Another, rather different way of asking the question is to ask whether there are evidential contexts in which our moral or passional nature ought to guide our beliefs; ought, that is, to contribute to forming those standards that determine what we ought to believe.

So I am not concerned here with whether, in a non-theoretical context in which there are less than ideal amounts of information, and in which people's interests and values are at stake, one ought or ought not to follow one's hunches. The question here is not, as it was for Pascal and also for William James, whether the non-theoretical interests of our moral nature ought to tip the balance in situations in which evidence is insufficient to warrant belief. I have no doubt that it can plausibly be argued that there are occasions when they ought. Rather, the question is whether there are kinds of evidence relevant to belief and unbelief which are filtered by one's moral nature. Ought we to use the evidence thus filtered by our moral nature as part of total evidence? Ought we to recognize that due to the influence of our moral nature we may have missed something?

I shall assume what I have argued for at length elsewhere,[9] that while there is a definite sense in which belief is not subject to the will, there is an equally definite sense in which it is. I shall assume that we each of us have belief policies, policies having to do with the epistemic and other standards for accepting and rejecting particular beliefs; and that we have the capacity to modify and replace those belief policies that we currently possess and use. If we ask questions of the general form 'What beliefs are we entitled to hold?,' then the general answer to such a question will be in the form of a belief pol-

---

[9] Paul Helm, *Belief Policies* (Cambridge, 1994).

icy: for example, that we are entitled to believe only those propositions which are more likely to be true than not; or that, as David
Hume put it, we shall be epistemically wise if we proportion our
belief to the evidence. Although Hume was firmly of the view that
beliefs are not subject to the will, he could hardly have said 'The wise
man proportions his belief to the evidence' unless he also held that
there is also a sense in which they are; and, like Hume, I think that
while single beliefs about straightforward matters of fact are not subject to the will, belief policies are.

FACTS AND VALUES: THEIR CONNECTEDNESS

It seems plausible that some types of theist should hold that there are
non-natural moral facts, such as facts about God's character and its
perfection, and even a realm of non-natural values which God gives
expression to in his various commands to the human race.[10] If God
is the sum of all perfection, the one who alone is worthy of worship,
then it seems plausible to suppose that among such perfections will
be moral qualities or properties. On such a view, without appreciating the fact of such properties, and their significance, one would not
appreciate what are essential aspects of God's character, and so one
would be in danger of seriously misunderstanding the idea of God.

While in the case of matters of empirical fact, facts are to be logically distinguished from values, in the case of God, or in the case of
some conceptions of God, the reverse is the case. It is true that there
are conceptions of God or of the divine which are expressed solely in
terms of power and intelligence. Let us call such a God a God of pure
power. But the God of the Judaeo-Christian tradition is not a God
of pure power but a God who also has a moral nature. If this God
exists, then not only does a being of immense power and intelligence
exist, but also a being of unsurpassable goodness, righteousness, and
love. Any conception of God for which the existence of evil is even a
prima facie problem is such a God.

We can express this point about the metaphysics of theism in various alternative ways. For example, if we have a strong doctrine of
divine simplicity we can say that while 'the goodness of God' differs

[10] For such a view, see, for example, Richard Swinburne, *The Coherence of Theism*
(Oxford, 1977).

in sense from 'the wisdom of God' or 'the power of God', these expressions have a common referent, the one indivisible being of God. This is a radical way of tying together the metaphysical and the moral character of God; the metaphysical and the moral are just different ways of referring to the one supremely divine being. Being supremely powerful implies being supremely good just because (in some rather obscure sense) the one *is* the other.

Alternatively, and less radically, we can articulate the idea in terms of essential properties. That is, God's nature may be best articulated in terms of property possession; among his essential properties, those without any of which he would not be God, are both (what we refer to as) metaphysical and moral properties. That is, we can say that among God's essential properties, along with omniscience and omnipotence, are goodness and benevolence and justice. The moral properties differ in character and meaning from the non-moral properties; neither, logically speaking, entails the other. So in this sense, at least, Hume's distinction between facts and values is preserved even in the case of metaphysical facts and moral facts, the metaphysical and moral properties which God possesses. Nevertheless, though neither logically entails the other, and thus it is logically possible (in the narrow sense) for there to be a God who is all-powerful but not all-good, nevertheless the nature of the God of Judaeo-Christian theism is such that God has both types of property, the metaphysical and the moral, essentially. The argument for this conclusion is either some idea of divine perfection, or what the Scriptures say about God, or some combination of these two factors. And of course, not only are these properties essential to God, but also God exists (in some sense) necessarily, either with necessity *a se*, or with metaphysical necessity of an even stronger kind.

However we articulate the point in detail, the basic idea is clear, that unlike matters of empirical fact, the matters with which the empirical sciences deal, which do not entail any matters of value, in the case of God value is, so to speak, built into his being. In enquiring into matters of empirical fact, in the interests of objectivity it is important to distinguish matters of fact from matters of value. It is important to recognize that from the fact that it is possible to explode atomic devices, or to perform abortions, or to tamper with genes, nothing follows as a matter of logic as to whether we ought or ought not to do any of these things. But in the case of both science and God, there are truths whether we like it or not. In the case of science, truths about atomic devices, abortions, and genes, say. In the case of God, truths about his nature and purposes. And in the case of God, some of these truths are moral truths.

One can put this contrast another way, as follows. Given the distinction between empirical facts and moral facts, matters of empirical fact do not have the power to cut across my moral interests. Of course, when these facts are put to use by human institutions then they most certainly do have that power. But then it is necessary to distinguish between the facts of physical nature and the uses to which those facts may be put; if you like, to distinguish between science on the one hand and the military-industrial or theological-ecclesiastical complexes on the other. From the fact that it is possible to make atomic devices it does not follow that they ought to be manufactured and exploded; nor does it follow that they ought not. From the fact that men and women can be burnt at the stake it does not follow that they ought to be; nor does it follow that they ought not. But it is the very distinction between empirical facts and moral facts that enables us to value or disvalue the empirical facts. Put paradoxically, matters of empirical fact as such cannot harm or help me; it is only when they are in my hands or in the hands of others, deployed in furtherance of some set of benign or malign ideals, that they affect my interests. But with the divine nature things are different: the values here are not in my own or another human being's hands, they are already in the hands of another, in the hands of the one who has them essentially.

So theology, or at least Christian theology, has important similarities and differences with the natural sciences. Like science, theology endeavours to be objective. It endeavours to draw conclusions about the existence and character of God and his dealings with the human race and the universe at large which are true, true whether or not anyone believes them, and whether we like it or not. Science handles data which are objective but morally neutral, though the use to which such scientific findings are put is not neutral in the same way. Theology, in a similar way, endeavours to establish facts which are objective but which include moral facts, facts both about God and about the proper goals and ideals of humankind.

What connection is there between the moral character of God and the moral character of the appraiser? There is, for example, the consideration of the connection between the putative acts of God and his moral character. For example, we can ask whether a certain moral code, or certain putative actions, are worthy of God. We may, as a result of investigating the moral character of God, be sure that certain types of human action cannot have been commanded by God; alternatively, we may as a result of such study come to a new appreciation of some action on coming to believe that it is commanded by God. We can fail to appreciate God's moral character correctly because of our own lack of moral insight, and so misdescribe God in crucial ways, even concluding (because of such misdescriptions) that God does not exist.

In coming to form beliefs about God's metaphysical and moral character one is concerned with crucial features of a world-view. In assessing world-views judgement, and not merely the assessment of empirical evidence, is called for. For we are dealing with theories or explanations or whatever that are total in character: theories of everything. One cannot therefore proceed inductively, and establish the reasonableness of a world-view a posteriori. I do not mean to deny that the usual canons of faithfulness to the facts, simplicity, and fruitfulness of explanation ought not to apply, but that it is much more difficult to apply these canons of rationality to world-views than it is to apply them to bits of the world. Many world-views, and certainly the Judaeo-Christian view of the world, have values built into them; and so in assessing their reasonableness one has to take into account not only facts that can be straightforwardly discerned by empirical means, but also moral values, whose means of discernment is less clear. In taking moral values into account one invariably discloses one's own moral values.

One might argue that in assessing questions which involve the issue of whether or not God exists the natural, whether metaphysical or empirical, ought always to take priority over the moral. But why?

So I wish to advance the following argument for consideration: judgements about what is true are affected by our moral nature; this nature is sometimes needed to evaluate evidence properly, and particularly situations in which there is evidence that is moral in character. *A fortiori*, a properly functioning moral nature is needed to evaluate evidence related to the existence and character of a God who has a moral character as part of his essential nature.[11] Here, I stress, I am concerned with the assessment of what one might call total systems of belief, rival world-views.

[11] On this point see Martha Nussbaum, *Poetic Justice* (Boston, 1995) and Robert C. Roberts, 'Emotions as Access to Religious Truths', *Faith and Philosophy*, 9 (1992), 83–94.

A situation might arise in which there is a conflict between evidence supplied to us by our moral nature, and evidence supplied to us by our senses. For as we have stressed, part of God's nature is non-naturally moral, part of what, objectively, there is. Therefore one needs to have a moral judgement, a moral sense, to appreciate this. An example from discussion of the problem of evil may help. When evidence is cited against the moral goodness of God, a moral judgement is made about the consistency of this evidence with the moral character of God. There are no further facts that are relevant, but a judgement is made (not by the accumulation of further empirical evidence) that the existing facts are inconsistent with that nature. It is not merely the putative logical inconsistency that is being judged here, but the character of God. There is only inconsistency, or only prima facie inconsistency, on a particular understanding of God's moral nature.

One might even extend the scope of those factors that may work in the establishing of the facts beyond our moral nature, to include the emotions. Ronald De Sousa has plausibly argued for an objectivist account of at least some emotions, or for emotions on some occasions.[12] Emotions may be aroused by objective states of affairs. Not all emotions are grounded in beliefs, but may themselves play epistemological roles. One such role that they may play, according to De Sousa, is to set the agenda for beliefs and desires: 'they ask the questions that judgment answers with beliefs and evaluate the prospects to which desire may or may not respond'.[13] Thus emotions may guide, or distort, the processes of reason; for example, we are most of the time curiously indifferent to our own death, but the prospect of death might alter a person's view of what is important and what not, so that he has a correct perspective on his life for the first time.[14]

There are types of explanation that integrate our experience and our view of the world from the centre outwards. These are not of course a priori explanation-types; but they are views which, though they arise partly from a consideration of the facts, and are susceptible to being modified by the facts, at least at the edges, are nevertheless attempts at explaining whole swathes of our life together; they are philosophies in a rather unfashionable sense of that word.

Scientific materialism is one such centre-outwards explanation, currently offering both a diachronic explanation, via the theory of

[12] Ronald De Sousa, *The Rationality of Emotion* (Cambridge, Mass., 1987).
[13] Ibid. 196.   [14] Ibid. 197.

evolution, and a synchronic explanation, via a theory of the unity of the mind and the brain, of all that happens to the human race, and to individual human beings. Of course materialism is not resistant to modification by the facts at the periphery, but it is highly resistant to overthrow by the facts. Perhaps such materialism is also the expression of certain values, for example that rational means of establishing matters of fact are appropriate to what we seek to control. However, I am not claiming that everyone can easily be convinced that there are integrative explanations of this sort. For there are intellectual tempers resistant to the attractions of such overall integrative explanations and which favour a piecemeal approach to all such problems.

The argument here is not against evidentialism as an epistemological theory; I am not claiming that there are non-evidential routes to knowledge. This is not an argument in support of fideism or irrationalism of any kind. But I am questioning the sole applicability of what I have called naturalist evidentialism to matters to do with reasonableness of theistic belief and arguing that our moral nature may sometimes be needed to properly evaluate the total evidence that is available to us, including the evidence for and of certain moral facts. We might miss or resist such evidence. That is, the argument is not that we can, by invoking our moral nature, justifiably ignore certain kinds of evidence, or justifiably leap the gaps in our evidence, but that our moral nature is needed to assess the total evidence, and so to assess the force of that evidence. Such a procedure is not inconsistent with attempting to be as objective as one's overall outlook permits. But it does involve allowing one's judgement to be affected by one's wants and interests, as well as requiring that one's wants and interests are kept under review.

OBJECTIONS

This is my claim: not only that our interests may delude us about the facts, through self-deception and fantasy, but that there are kinds of fact in a religion such as Christianity which are not straightforwardly empirical or metaphysical in character, but moral, and so are assessable not by our five senses, but by our moral nature.

I shall consider four objections to this thesis: it is too subjective; it is too objective; it is circular; it is Pharisaical.

First, it might be argued that despite what has been said earlier in defence of objectivity, what I am now proposing is at odds with it. To believe in accordance with one's wants and interests necessarily involves deceiving oneself about the evidence, pretending that the evidence is either stronger or weaker than it is, and so involves one in suppressing evidence. Such a stance is intellectually dishonest.

If that stance were required by the position that I am defending then it would be intellectually dishonest. But it is not. There seem to be two sorts of position that need distinguishing here. The first is the James-type position which, seeing that there are propositions which are not evidentially justified, nevertheless permits the passional nature to determine belief, or more precisely, the strength of belief, in such instances. The second is to think of the moral nature as ordering the evidence, as helping to evaluate its full strength and cogency. The first position we might call partial evidentialism; the second position is a full evidentialism but where evidence involves moral evidence. But neither need involve deception of oneself. It may be argued that whatever is impartially and disinterestedly assessed is more likely to be true than whatever is assessed by allowing full play to one's interests. This may be so, though one can dispassionately assess what is relevant to one's own interests.

A related argument is that believing in accordance with our moral natures impairs or weakens our truth-seeking capabilities, which ought to be as deeply embedded in us and as finely honed as they can be. But this objection is of relevance only if our moral natures have no cognitive capabilities. And if we are endeavouring to employ our moral nature to determine the real force of the evidence, it just begs the question against the position to say that it cannot be done.

An objection of the same general kind is as follows. It might be said that allowing our moral nature to determine what we believe cannot be distinguished from wishing; and wishing does not make it so. Conversely, empirical evidence is the best sign of truth, and as a belief is necessarily the belief that some proposition is true, belief ought to be conformed to the empirical evidence. The best sign of the fact that I have measles is that I have certain symptoms. Symptoms are reliable indicators. But the possession of such symptoms does not entail that I have measles. There is necessarily a contingent connection between evidence for p and the truth of p, where p is some empirical truth, though one cannot do better in estimating the truth or falsity of p than consider all the evidence that is relevant to p's truth. So—it might be objected—to suppose that a belief might be at least partly formed by non-empirical factors breaks the link between truth and the best sign of truth—empirical evidence. In response, no one doubts that a belief is true—or not—in virtue of the facts that are independent of the belief. But there is no reason why what our moral nature records might not, under certain circumstances and for certain purposes, be a sign of truth. For there may be lines of connection not only between scientific truth and empirical evidence, but between moral truths and the inclinations or disinclinations of our moral nature.

The second objection is from the threat of antinomianism. It might be said that objective, impartial enquiry is disciplined by the facts, but that this is not so in the case of morals. Our moral natures can be notoriously self-indulgent and therefore we ought to allow them no scope in the assessment of overall evidence. But this seems to be a counsel of despair. I cannot help myself reviewing what it is in my best interests to do. Why should consulting my moral values always be on the side of comfort and self-indulgence? May not moral considerations make demands which cut across my natural inclinations? Why may not *refusing* to consult moral considerations equally be on the side of comfort and self-indulgence?

A third objection is from the circularity of the appeal to one's moral nature. It might be objected that to rely upon one's own moral nature to evaluate the total evidence for the existence of God, or for some world-view of which the existence of God is an essential component, is a circular procedure. But there is no necessary connection between relying upon one's moral nature and drawing a particular conclusion. However, the deeper problem is that the appeal to moral nature appeals to evidence which pure empiricists do not believe can support the conclusion. So in trusting to the aid of their moral nature in their evaluation of the data as they see it, aren't such people implicitly taking it that theists are better judges of evidence than atheists? Aren't they proceeding by assuming the truth of theism, when it is theism that they claim they have evidence for?

But any such circularity is already present in areas of human enquiry in which apparently able investigators disagree about the overall force of complicated bodies of evidence.[15] Take two equally well-informed and competent observers who come to opposite or

[15] On this, see Peter van Inwagen, 'It is Wrong, Everywhere, Always, and for Anyone, to Believe Anything upon Insufficient Evidence', in Daniel Howard-Snyder and Jeff Jordan (eds.), *Faith, Freedom and Rationality* (London, 1996).

divergent conclusions about some complex historical matter. Each must assume that his own judgements about the relevant data, and the judgements of all who think like him, are sounder than those of his colleagues. The fact of deep divergencies in particular disciplines does not stop participants in those disciplines from having confident beliefs which they know are deeply disputed: in philosophy, say, beliefs about dualism versus monism; in history, disputes about the origins of the English Civil War; and so on. Furthermore, there is perhaps an *inevitability* in the use of moral nature in assessing total views, because a person's own interests are invariably involved in such views.

The final objection is that such a procedure can legitimately be accused of Pharisaism. The Pharisee of Jesus' parable thanked God that he was not as other men are; and there is a danger of Pharisaism, or at least of moral elitism, in the view that I have outlined. One attractive feature of the objectivity of science is its humility before the facts, and it may seem that to invoke moral considerations in the way I have been advocating is prideful. But the charge of Pharisaism can work both ways; it is certainly not the exclusive property of theists.

So I conclude, somewhat tentatively, that one may use moral considerations in evaluating total views; indeed, that it is impossible not to do so.

In an earlier chapter I distinguished between the cognitive or belief component of religious faith, and the fiducial element. If the conclusion of the argument of this chapter is reasonable then part of the cognitive content of the belief component of faith is sets of moral facts. So if the strength of the belief component of faith in God ought to be proportioned to the total evidence available, as I have been arguing, then that evidence will include evidence for the truth or falsity of certain moral claims.

6

'The Believer'

In our discussion so far we have concentrated attention almost wholly on the epistemic and evidential aspects of religious faith. We have argued that the belief component comprises beliefs of two sorts: beliefs about the cognitive content of the faith, which may involve an appreciation of moral facts, and beliefs about the believer's own needs and ideals. It has been argued that the cognitive content of the belief ought to be subject to a reasonableness requirement, though not one that violates the James Principle. It is, however, much less plausible to suppose that a person's goals and ideals might be subject to a reasonableness requirement of similar stringency. One might argue about the reasonableness of taking certain means to achieve certain goals, but it is harder to see how one can argue about the desirability or worthwhileness of incommensurable goals.

We have sampled two areas of current debate over the relation between faith and reason. In the second chapter we looked at rationality as it relates to issues about foundationalism, and in the third and fourth chapters we examined aspects of the connection between rationality, explanation, and the accumulation of evidence. In the last chapter we explored, more tentatively, the connection between a person's goals and ideals and the acquisition of evidence. I argued that not only can moral factors hinder or help the acquisition of relevant evidence, but they may also help or hinder the acquisition of moral evidence, the sort of evidence that is relevant to the question of whether it is reasonable or not to believe that there is a just and loving God.

In the first chapter I argued that on one reasonable understanding of what religious faith is (at least in the Judaeo-Christian tradition) it has not only an epistemic but also a fiducial component. Faith is in respect of this fiducial component an action, or action-like, in its character. For there to be faith there must not only be belief, there must also be the disposition of trust, the disposition to entrust oneself to another person or object. In this chapter we shall begin to shift our attention away from the purely evidential aspects of faith, those aspects which concern the belief component, to this fiducial aspect. While still maintaining our overriding concern with the rationality of religious belief, we shall consider not only the question of evidence narrowly considered, but also evidence when it is assessed in the light of the believer's own perceived needs and interests. For as we have seen, the action of trusting involves not only the believer's estimation of what is true but also what he believes to be of value or importance to him, and also the willingness to rely upon what he takes to be true.

In his discussion of ancient scepticism Myles Burnyeat has drawn attention to what he calls the 'practice of insulation'. He puts the point in the following way:

Nowadays, if a philosopher finds he cannot answer the philosophical question 'What is time?' or 'Is time real?', he applies for a research grant to work on the problem during next year's sabbatical. He does not suppose that the arrival of next year is actually in doubt. Alternatively, he may agree that any puzzlement about the nature of time, or any argument for doubting the reality of time, is in fact a puzzlement about, or an argument for doubting, the truth of the proposition that next year's sabbatical will come, but contend that this is of course a strictly theoretical or philosophical worry, not a worry that needs to be reckoned with in the ordinary business of life. Either way he *insulates* his ordinary first order judgements from the effects of his philosophizing.[1]

In the main part of this chapter I wish to look at one aspect of such insulation as it can occur in the philosophy of religion.

'THIN' AND 'THICK' BELIEF AND BELIEVING

Since the Enlightenment, perhaps since Descartes, what has come to be called the philosophy of religion has been centrally concerned with the reasonableness or unreasonableness of believing that there is a God. That issue has been the axis around which hundreds of books and papers have been written, and lectures delivered. Does God exist? Ought one to believe in God? Is it reasonable to believe

[1] Myles Burnyeat, 'The Sceptic in his Place and Time', in Richard Rorty, J. B. Schneewind, and Quentin Skinner (eds.), *Philosophy in History* (Cambridge, 1984), 225; italics his.

that God exists? These questions have been widely believed to express *the* issue which the philosophy of religion sets itself to address and even to settle, and this is still widely regarded as its sole proper task.

Someone who, in this context of thought, holds that God exists is conventionally called 'a believer'. He has a religious belief, he believes in God, he holds the belief that God exists, whether that belief is judged by him or by anyone else to be reasonable or unreasonable, warranted or unwarranted. Whether, like Kierkegaard, say, he holds that belief in God does not need to be reasonable, and perhaps cannot be reasonable, or, like William Paley, say, he holds that belief in God is more reasonable than not, the believer is forming his belief in the light of general canons of rationality, even if not in accordance with them.

When belief in God's existence is judged to be reasonable, the God believed in is almost invariably the God of the philosophers, the most perfect being. He is the God delivered to us by one or other of the proofs, or by the absence of any need to prove; he is the sum of perfection. As such he has various sublime attributes, including immense power and knowledge and an admirable moral character, and he is the creator of all that is, that necessary being on which all that is contingent depends.

One might, indeed, adopting a more austere view of natural theology, take such belief to an extreme by distinguishing between *that* God is from *what* God is. One might then argue that reason alone has to do with whether or not God, a necessary being, exists. Investigating the question of what God is like invariably takes us beyond the God of the philosophers to the God of religion.

We might justifiably and unsurprisingly say that the terms 'belief' and 'believer', as used in such contexts of natural theology, whether less or more austere, are epistemological terms. They have to do with the reality of God's existence and the grounds which make belief in that reality reasonable or otherwise, and with nothing else. Following James Ross, for reasons that I hope will become apparent, I shall call what is believed in such beliefs 'thin' theism,[2] and the associated belief or beliefs 'thin' belief.

One needs to distinguish between a thin belief and a belief with a thin content, between the act of believing and the propositional con-

---

[2] See James Ross, 'Cognitive Finality', in Linda Zagzebski (ed.), *Rational Faith* (Notre Dame, Ind., 1993), 228.

tent of the belief. Henceforward in this chapter I shall use some form of the verb 'to believe' to refer to the act of believing and refer to the propositional content as 'belief', and explore the relations between the two in respect of propositions about God. What I shall argue is that the God of the philosophers has a thin content and so belief in him can never be more than thin belief. By this I mean that though a person may sincerely and confidently believe in the God of the philosophers, and do so on what he takes to be good grounds, the propositional content of such a belief or beliefs is such that no practical response from the believer can reasonably be called for. Such believing can only be thin believing, for no action is called for either from believing or disbelieving. In this respect thin belief has a character like the belief that Hyperion is among Saturn's moons has for most of the human race. Nothing of any practical consequence follows from such a belief.

It won't do, I think, to say that such a person is cognitively indifferent to the propositional content of such belief, because these beliefs may have cognitive importance for him. In his philosophy, it may be important for some particular person that he can establish that the God of the philosophers exists, just as it may be important for an astronomer to know the names of Saturn's moons. Nevertheless the person may take up an attitude that is characteristic of all truly theoretical enquiry: what he knows he wishes to know for its own sake, and (where appropriate) he continues to keep an open mind on the truth or falsity of the belief. A person may hope or fear that a particular belief is true; but if he adopts a truly theoretical attitude towards that belief, then such hopes or fears will be sublimated to the ongoing, never completed processes of theoretical confirmation or disconfirmation. It may further such enquiry to hold the belief tenaciously, for after all he believes that he has good reasons for it, and such tenacity might provide motivation for retaining the theoretical attitude. Nevertheless, although such a person may not be cognitively indifferent with respect to p, he must be practically indifferent to it, since believing or not believing p carry no practical consequences, only cognitive consequences for others of his beliefs. However, although this is sufficient for thin belief, it is not a necessary condition for such belief, as we shall see.

Because of the cognitive content of beliefs about the God of classical natural theology, it is necessary that anyone who holds such beliefs about such a God, and only such beliefs about God, must take up an attitude of practical indifference with respect to the relevant propositions, and so believe thinly.

But there is a further sense of 'belief', and of the term 'believer', a sense that I shall argue is logically if not always temporally or historically separate from thin belief. In this second sense a believer is not only someone who believes that p, but who also trusts what p expresses or represents. He (or she) is someone who, believing that there is a God, also relies upon him. He believes in God in a different, though related, sense from that sense just discussed. God is, to such a believer, one who is eminently reliable, one to whom it is intelligible to make, or to refuse to make, a fiducial commitment. Of course the God of the philosophers, the God of our first context, is also reliable, but in a rather different sense. We might call this sense *conditional* reliability. Were the God of the philosophers to say something, to promise or to predict, say, then that promise or prediction would be reliable. However, though the God of the philosophers *could* promise or predict, there is never good reason to think that he might or that he does. And so he is not to be relied upon unconditionally. Though such a God is capable of making promises, for example, whether or not he has done so takes us beyond the God of natural theology. Let us call the theism which makes a range of responses such as trust, obedience, devotion, and rebellion intelligible and rational 'thick' theism, and the associated sense of belief 'thick' belief.

What are some of the other features of this second context of believing? One feature is that 'belief' is not solely epistemic, but also moral and fiducial in character. For what or who is trusted is not God abstractly conceived, the God of the philosophers, a necessary being, a God of supreme power and intelligence, for as we have seen it makes no sense to trust, or to distrust, such a God. Rather, what is trusted is what the thick believer takes to be the word or warrant or promise or covenant of God; something particular that, it is believed, God has done or said which calls for and warrants trust and reliance, or distrust and defiance. Taking up one or other of such stances involves the believer in estimating his own needs and goals, since what he takes God to have promised may or may not accord with what he wants. It is about this second sense of belief, belief as trust, that controversy raged at the time of the Reformation over whether faith alone justifies, that is, renders a person righteous before God. Is it sufficient, for justification, to trust God-in-Christ for it, or is more required?

In saying that the second sense of belief is primarily fiducial rather than epistemic in character I mean, of course, that it is both epistemic and fiducial. The second sense of belief presupposes a merely epistemic sense of belief, and evidence is necessary in such a case for such a belief to be rational. Thick belief entails belief that is cognitive in character, and empirical evidence or metaphysical argument (if it is a belief about an empirical matter of fact, or a metaphysical reality) is wholly appropriate to it. But it does not rely upon an account of knowledge and belief which is wholly theoretical in character, because it involves a person's beliefs about himself. In order to be justified in thickly believing that God exists one does not have to suspend belief while perusing the latest issue of *Faith and Philosophy* or *Religious Studies* in order to see whether what one previously thought was a valid, sound, and convincing argument for God's existence has turned out not to be.

The contrast that I am drawing between thin and thick belief has some similarities to that drawn by William James between a 'live' and a 'dead' option.[3] Yet the Jamesian distinction between the 'live' and the 'dead' cuts across my distinction between the 'thin' and the 'thick'. For an enquiry might be theoretically live but non-theoretically dead, as in the case of those many philosophers who have been interested in, say, the ontological argument from a purely professional viewpoint. Similarly an issue may be theoretically dead for a person but non-theoretically alive for that person.

We have distinguished between beliefs with a thin cognitive content, and beliefs with a thick content, and I have argued that thin believing is possible only in the first case, thick believing possible only in the second. But is thick believing necessary in the second case? One can, I shall argue, thinly believe in the God of religion, the God who is not only the perfect being of classical natural theology but also gives his word or covenant; but the character of such thin believing, and its explanation, is rather different than in the first case, thinly believing in the God who is purely the God of the philosophers. In the case of thin belief in the God of religion the believer is practically speaking indifferent to God's existence but he is not cognitively indifferent to it. Thick believing is only possible in a richer epistemic context than that of classical natural theology, but not all believing in such contexts must be thick believing. One can

---

[3] William James, 'The Will to Believe', in *The Will to Believe and Other Essays* (New York, 1917).

thinly believe in a situation where thick belief is also possible. One can have a detached and theoretical belief, a thin belief, in the God of religion. One can make the God who has promised or covenanted a matter of purely professional enquiry.

The thick believer may theoretically investigate those aspects of his belief capable of such investigation while continuing to be a thick believer. In such a situation one 'insulates', in Burnyeat's sense; belief remains thick belief, it does not transmute into indifference or distrust, while the propositions of such belief are subjected to theoretical enquiry, in rather the way the philosopher may investigate the nature of the external world while continuing to sit comfortably in his armchair. Insulation in Burnyeat's sense can occur only in a context where thick belief occurs.

The belief of the thick believer will include propositions held in common with the thin believer. The thick believer may also share some of the thin believer's evidence. But because thick belief introduces the practical concerns which we have discussed, the propositional content of thick belief is necessarily richer than for the central cases of thin belief, and the evidential standards applied to thick belief may be less rigorous than in the case of thin belief, because what matters for the reasonableness of such belief is not only evidence that it is true, but also the 'fit' between what the propositions of the faith offer, and the believer's own needs and aspirations. Indeed there is a kind of thick belief which separates itself from any evidential support whatever, in which the fiducial component refuses the offer of any evidential support, or can happily exist without it, and thus supplants any cognitive component of faith, as we shall see later.

So the thick sense of believing, the sense of believing which includes trust, may presuppose not only the beliefs held thinly by the theoreticians, the belief that the God of the philosophers exists, but other beliefs which make the thick belief intelligible and reasonable; alternatively, as we shall see, it is possible to have thick belief where there are no evidential grounds for such a belief.

Interesting further questions arise about the possible relations between thin and thick believing, and also about the co-presence of thin and thick believing. One question, as we have seen when discussing the practice of insulation, is whether a person could be both a thick believer and a thin believer with respect to the same proposition. And we have seen that there seems to be no insuperable reason why this may not occur, any more than there is any reason why a person may not be a theoretical sceptic but still, say, fly in aircraft. Burnyeat's insulating sceptic is like this. And as we have seen, someone could be a thick unbeliever but a thin believer. From a practical point of view a person could be an unbeliever, but be a believer when the question of whether or not God exists is faced as a theoretical issue.

There are other ways in which thin believing may be related to thick. For example it may be argued that thin believing is a necessary condition of thick belief: although the enquiries undertaken by the thin believer are never complete, they may attain practical certainty and enable thick belief to supervene. But later on in this chapter we shall find reason to doubt this. The same belief may be either thin and thick. The same belief may be held either as the result of a theoretical enquiry, or as a practical belief. A belief can be both thin and thick; A can believe p both thickly and thinly at the same time. However, more controversially, it might be claimed that no religious belief can be, or involve, thin belief. Some of the ways in which faith is held to be undiscussable that we examined in the first chapter might entail such a view. Conversely one might hold that no religious belief can be other than thinly held. But it might be hard to sustain such positions without stipulatively defining 'religion' in a conveniently appropriate way.

The converse of believing in God in the thick sense is not thin unbelieving, but thick unbelieving. A thick unbeliever displays distrust of God, and a range of responses with distrust as their centre, responses such as rebellion. Such distrust may take a number of forms. For example, it may take the form of a failure to thickly believe that what God says he will do he will in fact do. Such distrust is not disbelief in God's existence, but more like distrust in or distaste for God's character. Or it may be distrust in the sense that though God's character is regarded as trustworthy, what God has promised is not wanted. The devils, who, according to the Apostle James, believe and tremble, tremble *because* they believe, and they tremble because they do not want what God has promised, or perhaps, in their case, what he has threatened. The believer's exercise of thick belief is internally related to further beliefs about himself, about what he takes to be a good.

So the practical rationality of trusting God is compatible with any of several theoretical attitudes towards the existence of God, and certainly compatible with the failure to establish his existence in a theoretically watertight fashion. For this reason we may say that thick believing is *indifferent* to thin believing. It is because of this indifference that one can speak of the believer in the thick sense, but not the believer in the thin sense, as exercising trust, since the thin believer is concerned only with the project of theoretically establishing that God exists, never with trusting him. So faith in God as trust can only feature in thick contexts, since only such a context presupposes an interest not only in the existence of God but also in what he promises or commands.

Can one defend the overall rationality of thickly believing against the charge typically levelled against it by the person solely concerned with thin belief, that such belief is irrational, or not fully rational? Well, as we have seen, thick belief might build upon thin belief. But it needs also to be borne in mind that belief in the thick sense is practical belief, an act of reliance based upon certain beliefs and desires. As we have emphasized, trusting, which has both a cognitive and a fiducial component, is an action, or is an action-like activity; and it may be an action taken in the light of considerations that may be less than theoretically satisfactory, as most human actions must be. The standards of reasonableness of an action can be different from the standards of reasonableness of a belief.

If thick believing may be treated as an action, it can be expressed as the conclusion of a practical syllogism, as follows:

(*a*) I believe that whoever of trustworthy character invites one to trust him for something that one needs to rely on him for, then that person ought to be trusted.
(*b*) I believe that God is of such a trustworthy character.
(*c*) Therefore, I ought to trust God, in the sense of 'trust' which involves thick belief.

The conclusion of the syllogism is not that God is in fact trusted, but that he ought to be trusted. Such a distinction is appropriate because, as in all cases of practical reasoning, weakness of will may prevent what ought to be done from being done.

The exercise of faith, thick believing, requires an intentional object of trust. The intentional object of trust must be one the grounds for whose existence and trustworthiness are logically independent of the fact of trusting him. For even if God is eminently trustworthy, there is a logical difference between being trustworthy and being trusted.

It makes perfect sense to say of an object or person that it or she is trustworthy but not actually trusted. As we have noted, one explanation for why this might occur may be weakness of will; another may be a disvaluing of the object of trust.

So the two senses of believing that I have been outlining, 'thin' and 'thick' believing, are conceptually separable, because their occurrence is contingently related. Thick belief may occur in the absence of thin belief, and vice versa.

As we noted in an earlier chapter, it is said by some contemporary philosophers of religion that belief in God is *internally related* to a range of religious, ethical, and affective attitudes. By an internal relation is meant, I think, at least a relation of meaning. That is, it is frequently stated that if one is a believer in God it follows logically or conceptually, it 'makes sense to say', that one must take up certain attitudes, attitudes of reverence, worship, obedience, and so on, to the God believed in. Someone who allegedly believes in God but who does not take up one or other of these attitudes is said by such philosophers not to understand what it means to believe in God.

If by belief in God is here meant what we have identified as thick belief, then there is no problem about such internal relatedness, for trust or distrust in God certainly presupposes belief in his existence, and to trust is to take up a certain range of attitudes, weakness of will permitting. But as we have seen, thin belief in God's existence does not entail either that God is trusted or that he ought to be trusted.

The argument about the internal relatedness of belief in God to a set of actions is thus mistaken when taken as a comment on ordinary senses of 'belief' used in religious contexts. On the other hand, it may in fact be tacitly stipulating a particular sense of 'belief'; but if so, there is no need to accept the stipulation.

THE INSTABILITY OF THICK BELIEVING

There is one further interesting feature of thick religious believing that I should like to draw attention to. This is that it is inclined to be an unstable view, difficult to maintain, to keep up. I hazard the view that the tendency, certainly in those areas of Christianity with which I am most familiar, is for thick believing to disintegrate, to transmute into either thin believing, in which matters of belief are regarded as being of wholly theoretical interest, or into a purely fiducial or aspirational view of faith, according to which true religious faith is groundless trust or hope.

In the remainder of this chapter I shall endeavour to explore the prospect of such instability further by considering two different ways in which the supplanting of one sense of believing by the other has in fact occurred in discussion of the nature of faith. It has become a commonplace in much modern theology that because of the uncertainty inherent in theoretical enquiry, or because of some other rationally or empirically inspired consideration leading to uncertainty, the cognitive aspects of faith have been eliminated, or heavily downplayed, in favour of the fiducial, so that there is a real danger of the fiducial swallowing up or supplanting the cognitive, a danger which has not always been averted.

But before starting on this, I venture a general historical judgement. I believe that it is one of the legacies of Immanuel Kant's philosophical theology that the two contexts of belief that I have sketched, thin and thick belief, have so frequently become merged in modern discussions of belief and faith, and have had to be disentangled. They became merged for Kant himself, and there are at least two reasons for this: the first is that for him morality and religion are so intimately tied together; the second is that morality is for him a matter of rationality, and so the faith of a purely moral religion is an exercise of reason, albeit an exercise of practical reason.

So while Kant can find no place in religion for thin belief, considered as the outcome of a purely theoretical enquiry, but only for thin unbelief, or for the suspension of thin belief, he none the less has a place for religious belief as the outcome of a rational enquiry, namely the rational enquiry into what any person ought to do, a matter for Kant of pure practical reason. So the rationality of religious belief is necessarily that of practical rationality. Belief in God lies indispensably at the foundations of moral practice. So the distinction between thin and thick belief is totally inoperable in Kant and in all who have been significantly influenced by him. This is further underlined by the fact that for Kant no thick belief can have a component which could be the subject of theoretical enquiry. In so far as believing in God involves the exercise of practical rationality, then Kant's view of faith places it in the 'thick' category. In so far as thick believing involves a cognitive content rich enough to make practical rationality intelligible, Kant's view is not thick, since for him metaphysical theology is not available to human cognition.

In Kantianism it becomes impossible to prise apart God's existence, and belief in his existence, from his purely moral character, as the one, it is believed, who alone can make provision of the *summum bonum* for men and women in the life to come. A belief in God as the rewarder of moral virtue is not the outcome of an epistemological enquiry, it is a requirement of pure practical reason. For Kant the one and only thing which one can reckon that God does or will do, or at least can be rationally postulated of him, is to be the provider of the *summum bonum*, the rewarder of virtue and the punisher of vice. So God cannot fail to be trustworthy. For his existence is essentially connected—as a postulate of pure practical reason—with his character as a rewarder and provider in these precise senses and no other. So it is under the description of rewarder and provider that God's existence is rationally postulable according to Kant, and under no other description. As Kant is at pains to stress, such divine provision cannot be grounded in the historical, in occurrences in space and time, and there is no pre-mortem provision by God of any other possible kind. Rather it concerns the provision of the *summum bonum* in the life to come.

It is thus to Kant, rather than to the later Wittgenstein, that we owe the idea that belief in the reality of God may be an intrinsic part of a general conceptual scheme; in Kant's case, it is the scheme of morality, though he would not, of course, have expressed things in quite that way. Nevertheless God's existence has no rational basis outside the interests and requirements of morality. One might say that for Kant, belief in God is internally related to the adoption of certain moral duties, or at least to the intelligibility of wanting and intending to practise them. If one fails to believe in God (that is, fails to postulate his existence) then one has failed to understand both the character of morality and God's place in it. God has reality as a moral provider, and there is no other reason for supposing that he exists. For Kant the existence of God is internally related to the needs of this rational moral system.

Earlier I hazarded the view that thick religious belief is inherently unstable; it has the tendency to become either thin belief, or purely fiducial in character. We see one of these tendencies powerfully at work in Kant, the tendency of the non-cognitive, the practically rational in Kant's case, to swallow up the cognitive. In further support of my claim I offer two cases of a theologian and philosopher who illustrate the tendency for thick belief to transmute into a purely fiducial or aspirational view of faith. Examples of the opposite tendency, of thin belief's tendency to devour thick belief, could be given from the history of deism.

The first example is drawn directly from the neo-Kantian context, the case of Rudolf Bultmann. In his account of religious faith Bultmann conflates belief with trust, in the sense that for him trust expels belief, or totally supplants it; trust does all the work that, religiously speaking, belief once did, and now can no longer do, as well as doing its own work. So Bultmann offers to us a concept of religious faith or trust which does not logically require evidence of any kind. It is, in effect, a limiting case of thick belief in which no evidential component is present; trust requires belief, in the sense that it involves a certain kind of propositional attitude, but the belief that it requires cannot have any evidence in support of it or be susceptible to a lack of evidence. Religious belief thus has a propositional component, but no evidential component. Bultmann says,

Our radical attempt to demythologise the New Testament is in fact a perfect parallel to St. Paul's and Luther's doctrine of justification by faith alone apart from the works of the Law. Or rather, it carries this doctrine to its logical conclusion in the field of epistemology. Like the doctrine of justification it destroys every false security and every false demand for it on the part of man, whether he seeks it in his good works or in his ascertainable knowledge. The man who wishes to believe in God as his God must realise that he has nothing in his hand on which to base his faith. He is suspended in mid-air, and cannot demand a proof of the Word which addresses him. For the ground and object of faith are identical. Security can be found by abandoning all security, by being ready, as Luther put it, to plunge into inner darkness.[4]

Of course I am not concerned with whether this represents the whole of what Bultmann says on this matter, a rounded picture, nor with whether it is legitimate to extend St Paul's and Luther's theology in the way that he proposes, nor even with Bultmann's equation of evidence with proof. What I wish to draw out here is the consistency of such a view, the view, that is, that a man of faith is a man who necessarily trusts without evidence, without what Bultmann calls evidential security. Bultmann's proposal is that 'belief' or 'faith'

---

[4] Rudolf Bultmann, 'Bultmann Replies to his Critics', in *Kerygma and Myth*, i (London, 1972), 210–11.

in its primary Christian sense ought to be taken as a non-evidential concept. It has nothing to do with evidence, and as such it has no positive relation to the evidential paradigm of belief, thin belief. But because, in addition (for reasons that we need not identify here), Bultmann has no place for thick belief in the sense discussed earlier it cannot take the place of thin belief in his scheme. Bultmann's view of faith not only supplants thin belief, it supplants belief in any sense of that term for which it is appropriate to seek grounds for the truth of the belief. The fiducial, practical aspect of faith completely squeezes out the evidential aspect.

Such a view is certainly consistent, for Bultmann is not saying that faith has no object, which I think would not be cogent, but simply that any attempt to provide evidential support for that object would turn one's relationship with it into an evidential relationship, which would detract from its religious power, and would indeed be a form of idolatry. In Bultmann's eyes the search for such evidential support is tantamount to seeking justification by the works of the law, to seeking to obtain God's righteousness by works-righteousness, and it merits the same condemnation as St Paul gave to such activity.

The second case of the instability of thick belief is to be found, rather surprisingly, perhaps, in Professor Swinburne's treatment of faith in his book *Faith and Reason*.[5] Swinburne's motivation is rather different from Bultmann's, however.

A central place in chapter 4 of *Faith and Reason* is given over to a discussion of three views of faith, the Thomist, the Lutheran, and the Pragmatist views of faith, and to a critique of the Thomist and Lutheran views. In Swinburne's opinion it is a failure of each of the Thomist and Lutheran views of faith that they allow for something which, on his view, no satisfactory account of faith can allow for, that a scoundrel may be a man of faith. We shall consider Swinburne's account of the relation between faith and virtue in a later chapter. What concerns us here is what leads him to make the judgement that it is the Pragmatist view of faith which, all things considered, is the one to be preferred.

We have stressed that trust or trusting is an action. Swinburne agrees. For him trust is a voluntary action to which merit attaches, while belief (which Swinburne thinks of as a purely evidential notion, and as closely approximating to, if not identical with, thin belief) is

[5] Richard Swinburne, *Faith and Reason* (Oxford, 1981), ch. 4, 'The Nature of Faith'.

non-voluntary and so cannot be meritorious. For this reason the merit of faith cannot in any sense be a function of evidential belief, since the acquisition of a belief cannot be a matter of individual achievement. If faith is to be meritorious it cannot be a wholly evidential concept, but may only be minimally connected with belief-that, and may perhaps only be contingently connected with it, in that trust could exist without belief, and belief without trust. (In the terminology of the earlier part of this chapter, Swinburne would concur with the view that thick belief can exist without thin belief, and vice versa.)

For religious trust to be intelligible, and especially for it to be meritorious, which for Swinburne is both religiously and theologically desirable, it does not need to presuppose thin belief, or evidential belief of any kind; according to Swinburne, it only needs to presuppose *hope*, the hope that God exists, where such hope does not entail even the thin belief that it is more likely than not that he does. The man of Pragmatist faith is not so much the man of belief as the man of hopeful trust. On this view trust is not primarily a matter of belief, nor does it necessarily involve belief, but it is (in Swinburne's words) action with a good purpose guided by hope. Hope involves hoping for the fulfilment of some state of affairs, and this can be expressed in propositional terms, but it does not involve a belief that such a fulfilment will in fact occur.

So in the case of the Pragmatist view of faith, or in that version of it developed and endorsed by Professor Swinburne, the evidential content of belief, whether this is understood as the content of either thin or thick believing, is eliminated entirely, or almost entirely, in the interests of linking faith to action and so of safeguarding the place of human merit in religious faith or, as it becomes in Swinburne's account of Pragmatist faith, religious hope. The evidential component may in fact be a part of faith, but it is not an essential part. Although the genuine Pragmatist believer in God has to have some propositions which, naturally enough, he hopes are true, he does not have to have the propositional *belief* that there is a God, and *a fortiori* he does not have to have any *grounds* for holding such a belief.

The intellectual motivation for Swinburne's view is very different from that of Bultmann; indeed it comes from the other extreme of the theological spectrum. For Swinburne part of the reason for taking this view is to safeguard, in what we might call Roman Catholic fashion, the merit of faith. For Bultmann, it is, in robustly Lutheran fashion, to expel the very possibility of such merit in faith.[6] Nevertheless, the similarity between Bultmann and Swinburne at this point is striking.

Given Professor Swinburne's well-known stress on the need for the rigorous rational defence of the central tenets of Christianity, this result is rather surprising. It would be natural to expect that in his case at least the supplanting of thin belief by hope which he favours would go the other way, that the potential instability of thick belief would be resolved in the direction of thin belief. The man of faith would then be the man whose belief that God exists was evidentially well-grounded, or at the very least that such well-groundedness would be a necessary condition of faith. Why this does not appeal to Swinburne is due, philosophically speaking, to his involuntarist view of belief, as we have already noted, and to what, on theological grounds, he judges that the positive connection between faith and merit must be.

Earlier I mentioned that believing in God in the thick sense is related to certain ethical attitudes such that what believing in God partly means is having these attitudes, because the one trusted in has, in the eyes of the believer, supreme moral value, and has given enough information, by way of command, promise, or covenant, to make the notion of thick believing intelligible. What is Swinburne's position on the relation between belief in God and such moral and spiritual attitudes? He excludes the possibility of an immoral man being a man of faith not by arguing that thick belief is sufficient for the exclusion of immorality but by requiring that trust in his sense (i.e. acting on an assumption) be conjoined with a good purpose, and by even suggesting, in his account of Pragmatist faith, that the good purpose is the dominant element in faith. How trust in this sense, and acting on a good purpose, are to be conjoined, other than by an act of pure will or intention, is not made clear. We shall take up these matters in more detail in Chapter 8.

What these examples drawn from rather different philosophical and theological quarters illustrate is that there is a tendency for thick belief to split apart either into thin belief, in which the question of God's existence is considered solely as a theoretical issue, as in some

---

[6] It seems ludicrous to suppose that having certain beliefs could be a 'work', just as it is odd to suppose that faith, which according to the New Testament is a gift from God (Eph. 2. 8), could be meritorious.

forms of deism and in treatments of religion which regard it as solely a matter of academic enquiry, or into a purely fiducial or aspirational propositional attitude, an act of pure trust or hope.

Kierkegaard more than once remarks that to be a believer is like being suspended over 70,000 fathoms.[7] It seems to me that a better analogy is that the believer, the thick believer that is, balances on a tightrope, being always in danger of overbalancing in the direction of purely theoretical belief, thin belief, or purely fiducial belief, trust.

One possible response to this analysis of thick and thin belief, and the tendency of one to supplant the other, is that it rests upon a mistaken assumption, the assumption that belief in God is a case of belief in its common or garden-variety sense. One might imagine Rudolf Bultmann making such a retort, if not Professor Swinburne. If the *sui generis* character of religious faith or religious belief could be established, then this would be an effective retort to much of what I have been arguing. For religious faith being *sui generis* one might not expect it to be under the same kinds of evidential constraint as everyday faith, and so the question of thick versus thin belief as component parts of faith would not arise.

In the next chapter I shall argue that the claim that religious faith is *sui generis* has not been made out convincingly, and that this leaves us with the conclusion that the sort of trust with which one trusts God is the same kind of trust with which one trusts, say, a suspension bridge. Only the objects of trust, and the reasons for trusting, differ.

---

[7] For example, 'If I want to keep myself in faith, I must continually see to it that I hold fast to the objective uncertainty, see to it that in the objective uncertainty I am "out on 70,000 fathoms of water" and still have faith': Søren Kierkegaard, *Concluding Unscientific Postscript to 'Philosophical Fragments'*, ed. and trans. H. V. Hong and E. H. Hong (Princeton, NJ, 1992), 204. I owe this reference to Myron Penner.

7

What Is It to Trust God?

It may be argued that the whole business of trying to think of religious belief as a species of belief and religious faith as a species of trust, as we have been doing, is misplaced. Religious faith, it may be said, is *sui generis*, with its own rules, its own logic. If this is so, then the whole of our earlier discussion about the rationality of religious belief, and the relation of belief to faith, may be placed in jeopardy. This chapter is devoted to this question; and I shall argue that there is no reason to think that religious faith, and particularly the fiducial element in such faith, is *sui generis.*

So far we have focused upon the nature of faith, on some of the varying forms or concepts of faith, and their relationship to evidence. We have defended the idea that faith (in so far as it operates in Christianity) has both an evidential and a fiducial component, and that in a properly functioning religious faith the fiducial component is, *inter alia*, the outcome of both beliefs about certain objective matters of fact and certain beliefs held by the believer about himself. It has been argued that it is possible to offer defences of the reasonableness of religious belief, while allowing that there is a sense of 'faith' in which a person may have faith where there is no evidence. We have also argued that the rationality of adherence to a religion may be distinct from the rationality of holding a religious belief.

In this chapter we shall be concerned almost wholly with what it means to trust God, with the fiducial aspect of religious faith. In considering the belief aspect of religious faith I have assumed, rather than argued directly for, the view that it is univocal with belief used in non-religious contexts. In the present chapter I shall argue, consistently with this, that religious trust, the fiducial aspect of faith, is univocal with trust in other contexts. What distinguishes religious faith from faith in other things is the distinctive object of such faith, and the reasons that one has for exercising such faith and that alone.

One of the dominant elements in various kinds of modern theology is an emphasis upon the person. This personalist move in modern thought, and particularly in modern theology, goes back at least to Martin Buber (who wrote *I and Thou* in 1923) and to H. H. Farmer (*The World and God*, 1935) and John Macmurray (*The Self as Agent*, 1957), and includes figures such as Karl Heim (*God Transcendent*), Daniel Lamont (*Christ and the World of Thought*), Reinhold Niebuhr (*The Nature and Destiny of Man*), and William Temple (*Nature, Man and God*). This personalist movement has affected not only views of divine grace, but also of Christology, the nature of revelation, and (what is particularly of interest to us) the nature of faith. In some aspects of this general outlook the writers mentioned above were joined by Karl Barth and particularly by Emil Brunner (*Truth as Encounter*, 1938) and by a host of others influenced by existentialism. Such a trend was also supported by Boman's claim that Hebrew and Greek were different types of thinking, the Greek being allegedly objective, the Hebrew being intersubjective.

The sources of this trend are various; they lie in a critique of idealism, and also of individualism, and a denial to theology of a certain kind of objectivity, a point that was touched upon in the first chapter. One of the other objectives of this trend, it seems, was to head off reductionistic accounts of religion, for how could religion be reduced to anything else if it concerned a *sui generis* person-to-person relationship? It is intended by such claims to provide an a priori reply to the critique of the view that religion is an objectification or projection of human ideas and ideals. If personal relations are relations between two subjects, and at the heart of religion is a personal relationship between man and God, then man and God are and must always remain subjects. For the basic idea is that personal relations are relations between two subjects, not between a subject and an object. These subjects exist in mutual interaction. Perhaps lying further in the background of this network of ideas is Kant's doctrine of the two standpoints. It has even been claimed, as an extension of this personalist approach, that the doctrine of God as a trinity of persons offers illumination on matters as various as the idea of creation and of human community.[1]

One can hardly deny that persons differ from things, and that Christian theology deals with persons in relation. But there is more

---

[1] Colin E. Gunton, *The One, the Three and the Many* (Cambridge, 1993).

to the view under discussion than the endorsement of this common-place. When it is claimed that the relationship between a human person and God, and between one human person and another, are cases of an I–Thou relationship, and that to trust a 'thou' is different from trusting an 'it', I shall take it that these are intended to be ways of identifying different *kinds* of trust. Otherwise it is hard to see where the distinctiveness of personal trust lies. So in what follows I shall assume that what is being claimed is that to trust a person is to engage in a different *kind* of activity from that of trusting any thing that is not a person. These two different types of activity no doubt have features in common—otherwise it would be inappropriate to refer to them both as cases of trust—but neither is a case of the other, any more than the activity of curling a stone is the same activity as curling a head of hair. The question then is, does the idea of persons in relation provide us with a different category of enquiry, and call for the formulation of a different conceptual apparatus to deal with it? I shall argue that no good reasons have been offered for thinking that it does.

Undoubtedly the *phenomenology* of trusting God differs from that of trusting the efficacy of a drug, or from trusting one's teenage son to return safely in the car; such differences are no doubt due to the respective intentional objects of the trusting, in rather the way that the phenomenology of fearing a rise in inflation differs from fearing the oncoming pit bull terrier. In particular the phenomenology of trusting people is different from that of trusting things because in trusting another person I am trusting someone who may or may not trust me. Not only am I a subject, I am or may be someone else's intentional object. Even as I trust the other person I can be looked at, weighed up, and responded to by him. In a word, I am aware of another person, and he may be aware of me. No doubt this aspect of interpersonal relations is strong in most accounts of trusting God. Nothing that follows will attempt to deny this. But by itself this fact does not show very much about the distinctiveness of personal rela-tions. For the fear that I have of the pit bull terrier's approach arises because I am, or may be, the terrier's intentional object.

It is certainly a reasonable claim, and one which I do not in any way wish to dispute, that the source of a person's trust in God, and what that person trusts God for, may be distinctively different from the sources of trust in all other cases. As my trust in a drug may be expressed in appropriate kinds of attitudes, and these kinds of attitudes mostly differ from those attitudes exhibited when I trust a person, so my trust in a person, another human being, may differ from my trust in God though it is not, of course, altogether different. Other people are trusted for different things, and in different ways, from the things for which God is trusted and the circumstances in which he is trusted. So what makes one case of trust different from another is something about the belief component in faith, namely the different possible intentional objects of such belief.

Despite these readily acknowledged and important differences, I shall argue that there is good reason to suppose that the concept of trust in each case may be univocal. Trusting God may be like trusting anything else one trusts. I shall call this the *sameness thesis.* Its denial I shall call the *difference thesis.*

In what follows I shall start by examining two or three conceptual preconditions of trust, but then spend the remainder of the chapter defending the view just stated against the strongest objections that I can think of. I do things in this way for two reasons. One is that it seems obvious to me that the sameness thesis is correct, and so I am naturally both inquisitive about and sceptical of the cogency of any reasons that may be given for denying it. Indeed, one reason I have for discussing this topic is surprise that the difference thesis is so often held as if it were obvious, and as if scepticism about it is absurd, betraying a fundamental failure of insight. The second, less autobiographical reason for structuring the discussion in this way is that since the same word is used in the same sense to express reliance upon a drug, a piece of rope, one's wife, and God, there is at least a prima facie reason to suppose that the sameness thesis is true. Hence the burden of proof must be on those who think that trusting God and trusting human beings is a different *kind* of trust.

CONCEPTUAL PRECONDITIONS

A brief word first about conceptual preconditions of an interpersonal relation of trust on the side of God. There are certain conceptions of God—so it seems to me—in which it would be difficult, if not impossible, to think of anyone being in a relation of trust to such a God; they would, at best, thinly believe in such a God. A God whom one had good grounds for believing had created the world as a self-sufficient physical system, and done nothing more, would not need to be trusted, or only barely so; perhaps trusted to keep the system going, but no more. But as we saw in the last chapter, religious trust, involving thick belief, occurs more readily when God is believed to be more engaged with human happenings that he is in such deism; when he has revealed his purposes for mankind, or when he has made promises to men and women, or entered into covenant with them, or when people believe that he has done any of these things. And so I shall take trusting God to fulfil what he is believed to have promised to be a central case of trusting God.

It might be thought that here are already present the seeds of the allegedly crucial distinction between trusting people and trusting things. For if a central case of trusting God is trusting his promises then it will be quickly pointed out that promise-making is a distinctively personal activity. Bridges and drugs and horses may each be trusted, but they cannot issue promises and so cannot be trusted as another human being or as God is trusted. While this is true, I think that these differences can be narrowed, and may even be overcome completely. In trusting the bridge one trusts some fact or state of affairs about the bridge which can be expressed in a proposition; say, the proposition that the bridge will take my weight. This proposition is not of course uttered by the bridge, nor is it in typical cases separately identified in consciousness as we are now identifying it. But the proposition about the bridge on which trust is based is, in the typical case, grounded in evidence manifested by the bridge and believed to be true of it. In the case of trusting people, including trusting God, the propositions are separately identified as utterances or inscriptions. But the fact that they *are* separately identified does not mean that their creditworthiness is to be established separately from that of the utterer. A person's promise is trustworthy because the person is trustworthy. Though the promise is separately identifiable, it does not have a separate identity as a trustworthy promise. The promise of God is a manifest feature of his life in the same way as the solid structure of the bridge is one of its manifest features which makes it reasonable to trust it.

The relation between the promiser and the promise is seen by the fact that in order to believe the promise the believer has normally to make reference to the intention and the character of the utterer in making the promise—whether he is intending the words seriously, or as a joke, for example—in order to be sure that what he has uttered is a promise and that he is in a position to keep it. So the difference between trusting God (or trusting any person) and trusting a bridge cannot be established simply by pointing out that bridges cannot make promises. Bridges do not make promises, but in appraising the bridge's trustworthiness there is something akin to appraising a person, namely investigating whether what appears to be a feature of the bridge making for its trustworthiness is in fact a feature making for its trustworthiness.

A second conceptual precondition of interpersonal trust has already been hinted at. It is that trust involves a set of propositional attitudes. This is because, as I have argued in earlier chapters, a necessary condition of reasonable trust is reasonable belief. So to trust the bridge, or at least for trust in the bridge to be reasonable, it must entail the reasonable belief that the planks which the bridge is made of will bear my weight; for trust in God to save my soul to be reasonable entails the reasonable belief that God can save my soul; the trust may vary in strength as a person's grounds for his belief may vary.

A third precondition relates to trust and desire. Take the following case. A wife may take very seriously her husband's threats to beat her because of his past behaviour. He has beaten her in the past, and he is invariably as good as his word. When he says that he will beat her, he does beat her. She gives good evidence that she believes his threats by fleeing the house. But in these circumstances she could hardly be said to trust him; quite the reverse. She believes his word and acts upon it but does not trust him. What makes the difference? Just this, that trust is trust for good, or for what the one who trusts takes (perhaps mistakenly) to be good. The wife believes her husband and for that reason refuses to entrust herself to him.

As I argued in the first chapter, for trust to be rational it must involve evidence, though I recognize that views differ on this, and also recognize that there are irrational forms of trust which do not involve evidence and may even involve the repudiation of evidence. The relation between trust and evidence will surface again later in the chapter.

So much for the conceptual preconditions of interpersonal trust, my starting point. I shall now consider four arguments in support of the difference thesis, the thesis that trusting God is a different kind of trust from trusting the bridge. The first two of these arguments share a common assumption, that trusting God is a case of personal trust, and so the arguments are couched in terms of trusting a person rather than trusting God. I shall call these four arguments the argument from *interests*, from *interpersonality*, from *God and evidence*, and from *bare particularity*.

INTERESTS

Let us suppose that there is a categorical difference between trust in persons and trust in things, and that since God is a person, trusting him must be different from some other kinds of trust. And further, let us suppose that what is peculiar to such trust in persons is that it has a moral character, involving the mutual recognition of obligations, or the recognition of privilege and responsibility. While it makes no sense, for example, to trust the integrity of a horse or a drug, or to trust them because of their integrity, it makes perfect sense to talk about trusting the integrity of my friend, trusting him on account of his integrity, and *a fortiori* it makes sense to trust God on account of his integrity.

I think that the point being made by such claims is the following. One may have good grounds for trusting in the integrity of a person without being able to anticipate where such trust will lead. To have integrity in this sense is to have a set of principles which are closely unified and which one abides by. I may not see how a person whose integrity I trust (say, in a complicated set of financial dealings) will advise and act. It is my very inability that leads me to trust him and not to attempt to work things out for myself. Nevertheless I believe that he will propose some course of action which is consistent and honourable, even though it may be unexpected. So in trusting such a person I go out on a limb, I entrust myself to him, over a range of matters the extent of which I cannot now anticipate. Furthermore, even in matters which I can anticipate, I may not be able to anticipate how that person's integrity will be expressed in handling these matters for me. In trusting I entrust myself, or a part of myself represented by certain of my interests, to another.

This argument makes the point, to be discussed more fully in considering the second argument, that relationships between people are responsive, reciprocal relations, or potentially so. Unlike my relationship to the bridge, or the drug, another person is only capable of receiving my trust because I believe that he is capable of responding in appropriate ways to me, or on my behalf. Hence it is crucial for the appropriate trusting of another person that whoever trusts that person has beliefs about that person's intentions.

Someone who took this line, insisting on the moral aspect of interpersonal trust, might at this point simply insist on the reasonable point that people have a moral standing in a way in which bridges and drugs necessarily do not. But the interesting question is: what is it about such responsiveness that crucially affects the trust? Why does its being or involving a moral relationship affect its character as trust?

Consider a range of cases: trusting a bridge, a drug, a dog, a horse, a small child. In each case trust may involve entrusting oneself to a differing and perhaps an enlarging range of powers. What one can trust a bridge for or with is more restricted, but also different, from what one can trust a horse for or with, and so on. And in the case of a person, unlike a bridge or a drug or a horse, that person can have your trust in them as a reason for behaving in some particular way towards you. But the presence of such mutuality is a matter of degree, and the moral relationship between truster and trusted may not be proportional to this degree. But then how is the point about a moral relationship relevant? It simply reduces to the fact of mutuality, which is, as I said, a matter of degree and not of kind.

The allegedly distinctive trust in a person (as opposed to trust in something which is not a person) is either founded on the moral status of that person, or on the exercise of mutual relations. Just as having the moral status of a person is (we might allow) an all-or-nothing affair (one cannot be half or two-thirds a person) so trust in anyone that has that status must be an all-or-nothing affair, and in no way is to be compared to the trust one has in, say, a horse or a recipe. However, if distinctive personal trust is based on the exercise of mutual relations then, since such exercise is a matter of degree and is continuous as between persons and non-persons, such trust must also be a matter of degree. In any case, it is just false to suppose that the degree of one's trust in another person may not diminish or increase. But there appears to be a contingent connection between the moral status of a person and the scope for trusting that person. If so, then the scope that there is for trusting a person must be a function of other things besides their moral status. Hence trust would not have to do only with the moral status of the one who is trusted.

There is a variant of this position, which can be expressed as follows. The point about trust, it is sometimes said, is that it goes beyond reliance upon what people do, and centres upon the people themselves. Here trust does not involve the denial that it is a propositional attitude; rather it is claimed that trust supplants the propositions of such attitudes. So it is frequently said that there is more to trust than reliance upon what can be expressed in terms of a set of propositions, because there is always more to a person than sets of such propositions.

Such a point does, I believe, capture something of the essence of trust. But I doubt that the point is sufficiently strong to drive a permanent wedge between trusting people and trusting things. What do I mean? When you trust another person you trust someone who is capable of taking initiatives, and these initiatives may be at the expense of one's own interests, or indifferent to them, or supportive of them. In trusting a person, therefore, one is relying upon what that person has yet to do, a potential. What may tempt us to regard the trust of a person as distinctive is the *range* of such potentials. For a horse can also be trusted in precisely the same sense, trusted for the exercise of certain of its abilities should the need for that exercise arise. The only relevant difference is that in the case of the horse the range of potential activities which may vindicate my trust in it is different from that in the case of trust of persons. So I may entrust myself to the horse, and also the horse may respond to my trust because it senses it. Here there is a relation of trust which involves responsiveness, but in which only one of the partners is a person.

What one trusts in another person or thing is the reliable exercise of, or the reliable disposition to exercise, certain powers and capacities. One trusts the drug to react in a clinically favourable and predictable way; to control the symptoms of Parkinson's Disease, say. One trusts a recipe to ensure that a perfect soufflé is created. To trust that the agent, whether intelligent or inanimate, will exercise the appropriate powers is to trust the agent to exercise those powers under relevantly similar circumstances. But it is surely implausible to suppose that corresponding to each set of powers there is a distinctive kind of trust.

A reply to this argument might be made along the following lines. It might be claimed that what makes trust distinctively personal is that it is unconditional. In 'Moral Judgment, Action and Emotion'[2]

[2] Bernard Harrison, 'Moral Judgment, Action and Emotion', *Philosophy*, 59 (1984), 295–322.

Bernard Harrison offers an argument in defence of the *sui generis* character of personal trust. He says that what '*A* trusts *B*' means is that *A* is willing to rely unconditionally on *B*'s unwillingness to allow any justified convention-backed claim of *A*'s to be neglected or over-ridden.[3]

This is an intended characterization of unconditional, i.e. unreserved, trust in someone about a matter. It is not what might be called total unconditional trust, trust in *B* with regard to anything of *B*'s which has or might have an impact on *A*. This Harrison makes clear with the example of full-bloodedly trusting someone with respect to some particular activity; not to cheat at cards, say.[4] He further says that what makes trust full-blooded is that in trusting *B*, *A* has the belief that *B*'s trustworthiness does not derive from *B*'s calculation of his own interests, or from any character traits not controllable by *B*, but from a voluntary and settled commitment of will on *B*'s part.

Harrison seems to be supposing a situation in which the character traits that *B* has which are not controllable by him can play no part in *B*'s trustworthiness. But such trustworthiness surely has grounds; it is, or may be, reasonable for *A* to trust *B*. And when it is reasonable then surely this trust is grounded in features of *B*'s personality some of which, at least, may be traits over which *B* has no immediate control.

So Harrison does not appear to have shown that the rationality of *A*'s unconditional reliance upon *B* cannot be grounded, in part at least, in uncontrollable traits possessed by *B*. And since such trust is grounded partly in such traits, it is hard to see how full-blooded trust, which Harrison thinks is characteristic of interpersonal trust, differs qualitatively from other kinds of trust. And in any case, even if we allow Harrison the point, such an account of trust would not easily transfer to the case of trusting God, for presumably the rationality of such trust lies in the character of God, and it is highly unorthodox, if not incoherent, to suppose that God could choose to alter his property of, say, being immutably faithful to his promises.

---

[3] Ibid. 311.
[4] Ibid.

INTERPERSONAL RELATIONS

It might be argued that what is distinctive of human interpersonal relations, including interpersonal relations between God and man, is that each is capable of loving the other, and that trust is an aspect of love, and that love is only possible where two people are indeterministically free with respect to the other. The argument might go as follows:

(1) Trust as an interpersonal relation is to be distinguished from trust in non-personal things.
(2) Interpersonal relations require mutual indeterminism.
(3) God and man are each indeterministic agents.
(4) Therefore God and man are capable of entering into interpersonal relations such as trust.
(5) Therefore a person's trust in God is to be distinguished from that person's trust in things.

One finds an argument like this in a number of the writings of Vincent Brümmer.[5] The problem I have with such a position concerns how it is possible for the metaphysics of indeterminism to enter into the argument. By this I do not mean that I have doubts about the claimed mutual indeterminism, though I have, but that granted such indeterminism it is difficult to see how it is relevant.

The only plausible way that I can think of in which mutual indeterminism is relevant to the claim that interpersonal relations are *sui generis* is via what the partners in dialogue believe about each other. What the argument would then amount to is the claim that if the persons in question do not believe in the causal indeterminacy of relevant pieces of behaviour of their partners then they will not be able to trust them.

But the problem with invoking such belief, and of giving it a role in the understanding of trust, is plain. In fact it is a twofold problem. One difficulty is that the fact that a person may believe that he and his partners in some activity are indeterministically free does not

---

[5] For example, *What are we Doing when we Pray?* (London, 1984) and *Speaking of a Personal God* (Cambridge, 1992). I have discussed further aspects of this issue in 'Prayer and Providence', in Gijsbert van den Brink, Luco J. van den Brom, and Marcel Sarot (eds.), *Christian Faith and Philosophical Theology* (Kampen, Netherlands, 1992), 103–15.

entail that they are. So interpersonal trust might be founded on an illusion. But equally seriously, is there evidence that people who trust each other also do in fact believe that they are indeterministically free, and that they are able to exercise such trust only because they are indeterministically free? It does not seem likely. It does not seem likely that everyone, from small children upward, who exercise interpersonal trust have such sophisticated metaphysical beliefs about themselves and others.

It might be replied that this does not matter in the least. What matters is what the truth-conditions for personal trust are, not whether or not those engaged in personal trust are aware of those conditions. My heart does not function only when I understand what makes it function. And what is true, the reply might continue, is that trust is an interpersonal relation in the sense described, whatever the truster and the trusted may or may not think.

This claim is that it is important to distinguish, in trying to understand such concepts as trust, between the conditions which have to be true for something to be a case of trust, and what the truster has to believe about the one he is trusting in order for him to be genuinely trusting that person. To revert to our previous argument, it might be said that when Harrison cites, among the conditions of full-blooded trust, the condition that the truster must believe that B's unwillingness derives neither from B's calculation of his own interests, nor from desires or character traits over which B has no control,[6] he is in fact specifying truth-conditions for such trust and not conditions that must be believed by the one who trusts in order to ensure genuine trust.

If, for example, someone were tempted to found the distinctiveness of trust in persons as opposed to things on a Reidian or Swinburnian view of the self, on the idea of the self as a simple and unanalysable ego, then it would be appropriate to respond that what matters for trust is not that those who trust have such a view of the self, but only that those who trust and are trusted are cases of such selves. Let us call this the externalist standpoint on trust.

I do not think that the externalist standpoint is plausible in such cases. For our discussion concerns the phenomenological character of trust, with how trust *seems* to those who trust. How trust seems involves what beliefs those who exercise trust must necessarily have,

---

[6] Harrison, 'Moral Judgment, Action and Emotion', 311.

and a person's relationship with those beliefs. And since we are dealing with the psychological 'surface' of trust, how trust seems is crucial for understanding how it is, i.e. what trust is. The parallel with the contrast between internalist and externalist accounts of epistemic justification does not hold, since whatever the difference may be between two kinds of trust that difference must be fairly easy for trusters to recognize. Perhaps the features are not part of the phenomenology of trusting, its felt character, but are part of the dispositional structure of trusting, such that if the truster were asked whether a case of trusting a person differs from a case of trusting a thing, and asked what the difference is, he would be able to offer an answer, and all trusters would be able to offer more or less the same account.

Of course if the distinction between trusting persons and trusting things were an unimportant feature of trust we could afford to neglect it. But according to the view being discussed, there is an essential difference between the two. It would thus be reasonable to expect those who are capable of exercising or withholding trust, who in this sense have a mastery of the concept of trust, to recognize the distinction, and to recognize that there are or might be occasions when they mistakenly entrust themselves to things in a way that is only appropriate to entrusting themselves to persons, and vice versa.

It is possible to sharpen up this objection to the externalist standpoint by putting it in the form of a dilemma: either genuine full-blooded personal trust requires the fulfilment of conditions about the nature of personality (I use this as a portmanteau term for all that has gone before) or it does not. If it does then only those who can grasp such conditions can exercise full-blooded trust. If it does not then a person may genuinely trust a person or a thing without being able to distinguish the two different kinds of trust. And I have been arguing that the internalist standpoint is appropriate but that it is implausible to suppose that all those who genuinely exercise trust have a grasp of the sophisticated theoretical concepts, such as the difference between determinism and indeterminism, referred to by those who wish to make a sharp distinction between trusting people and trusting things, and *a fortiori* a sharp distinction between trusting things and trusting God.

GOD AND EVIDENCE

So far we have considered two arguments each of which concerns the case of trusting God indirectly, via the broader concept of a person and what is involved in trusting a person. But of course God is by definition unique. And it might be alleged that trusting God is *sui generis* because God is in a unique metaphysical position and so in a unique epistemic position.

I shall take as an example of such a possible approach a paper on faith and evidence by O. K. Bouwsma.

What is characteristic of Bouwsma's approach is that he holds that there *cannot* be evidence for the central tenets of Christianity. The impossibility is not, he maintains, a physical impossibility, nor is it epistemic. It is not that we cannot reach God as we cannot reach the outskirts of the physical universe; nor is the impossibility due to the fact that we do not know where to look or what would count as evidence. The impossibility in question is the impossibility of there being evidence for such matters as the existence of God, or for any of his deeds.

Bouwsma distinguishes between the divine and human elements in biblical history; there can be evidence for the human element, but not for the divine, so that faith in God is faith in a proposition or promise for which there could not be evidence.

I am interested in emphasising that the religious belief of Abraham, namely, that God commanded him to go and promised him a future, this belief is of an altogether different order. For this there can be no evidence. I dare scarcely say that we can understand this, I mean, understand what Abraham believed.[7]

Later in the same paper, writing of Jehovah's appearance to Moses at the burning bush, he writes,

Belief is possible. And such belief! Is there now no evidence possible that the angel of Jehovah appeared to him in a flame of fire? There is no evidence and no evidence possible. It is not that evidence is lacking. Evidence is inconceivable.[8]

[7] O. K. Bouwsma, 'Faith, Evidence and Proof', in *Without Proof or Evidence: Essays of O. K. Bouwsma*, ed. J. L. Craft and R. Hustwit (Lincoln, Nebr., 1984), 9. I have discussed Bouwsma's paper from a rather different point of view in *Belief Policies* (Cambridge, 1994), 202–7.

[8] Bouwsma, 'Faith, Evidence and Proof', 11.

And again,

And what is the evidence? Admitting, however, that the urge to persist in this question, almost as though one scanned the landscape to search for the evidence, is extremely powerful, the problem arises as to how it is that we do this. It is not, remember, that we can look for what is not there. Neither is it like looking for air in a vacuum. There might be air in the enclosure which is supposed to be a vacuum. It is rather like looking for air in joy, in kindness, in anger. It is said that oil and water do not mix. And so it is with evidence and faith.[9]

So Bouwsma holds that there are cases of belief or faith for which evidence is impossible, and that these are the exemplary cases of religious belief or trust. Bouwsma cites paradigm cases of faith as far as Christianity is concerned: Abraham and Moses and Paul. It may be that he would say that such cases are of belief 'in', belief in God, or even of believing God, rather than of belief 'that'. But there is no reason to think that he would deny that such cases involve beliefs 'that'—the belief that God exists, for example.

So what, according to Bouwsma, is characteristic of faith, faith in God, is not simply that it is a trustful, fiduciary relationship, but that it is such a relationship in a situation in which there could not be evidence for (nor, presumably, evidence against) the object of trust. Bouwsma gives two main reasons for taking this position. I shall call these the ontological and the religious reasons. The ontological reason has to do with the fact that God is not a part of the physical universe, and cannot be.

We are like people who lie in an enclosure behind walls, and the question 'Is there a God or not?' is a question about what is behind the wall.[10]

So for Bouwsma nothing in the universe can provide evidence for (or against) whatever is outside the universe. Evidence is only relevant in cases which are 'analogous to cases in which we know both what corresponds to the evidence in this case and what we come to know by way of that evidence'.[11] And presumably whatever is outside the universe is God; even angels are creatures. Perhaps evidence for such creatures is thin, perhaps there is no evidence at all. But if it is impossible to gain evidence of angels this is not impossible for the same reason that it is impossible to gain evidence for God's existence. One *cannot* have evidence for God, the divine mind, who is distinct from the universe, as one can, say, for creaturely minds.

[9] Ibid. 18.   [10] Ibid. 4.   [11] Ibid. 7.

The religious reason provided by Bouwsma has to do with the relationship between evidence and trust. About evidence we can ask how much there is, whether the evidence could be better, whether it has been properly weighed, and so on. But

> We are not to say that since Abraham believed that God called him and that God promised, it must be so or very likely to be so. . . . The Scriptures say, 'And Abraham went', and later, 'And Abraham believed'. They do not say, 'After having taken all the reasonable precautions about being taken in and after making sure that he would be able to give a good account of himself to his friends, he decided to obey the order'.[12]

So there is something *sui generis* about true religious belief. Such belief is conceptually connected with obedience:

> 'Who art thou, Lord?' is said by one who in saying it does not make a discovery, as though he noticed something and inferred that Jesus was after all someone important, perhaps Moses or Elijah, as men had said earlier. In this utterance Saul becomes a servant, certainly not knowing what the end would be, and as he would have said, 'through the grace of God'. It is a mistake to regard Saul as believing at one moment and obeying the next—as though he then said, 'Well, I had better'.[13]

So Bouwsma is saying that there is a non-contingent connection between belief in God, trust in him, and obedience. On this view it is most certainly the case that trust in God is not, and cannot be, like trusting the plank or the drug. We may even say that trust in God is *necessarily* not like trust in these things, nor like trust in any other person. Because of who God is, trust in him must be unlike trust in anything else.

What are we to say of this argument for the view that religious faith is trusting a person, God, and not trusting a thing? It clearly *is* an argument for this conclusion, and is intended to be a strong argument. For what Bouwsma implies is that both trust in a non-person and trust in all creaturely persons is trust which requires evidence; but trust in God is different. Hence there is one case of personal trust, namely trust in God, which is different from all other cases of trust. So Bouwsma is not maintaining the thesis that trust in God is personal but that some cases of trust in persons are distinct from all other cases of trust. This is a theory not of trusting persons but of trusting a *divine* person.

---

[12] Ibid. 8.   [13] Ibid. 12–13.

What are we to say to it? I shall offer an argument or two to cast doubt on what Bouwsma claims.

There is, to begin with, a difference between saying that we do not or cannot now have the evidence which Abraham had when God called him, and saying that Abraham could not have had evidence and did not. Even if the first is correct, the second may reasonably be doubted. Bouwsma appears to want to say both, but one is distinct from the other, and the fact that we cannot be in Abraham's position does not imply that Abraham could not have evidence for his trust in God's promise.

Further, it seems to me that not only *could* Abraham have evidence but that, *pace* Bouwsma, he *did* have evidence. I offer these two reasons. Bouwsma supposes that Jehovah said to Abraham, 'Get thee out . . .' Let us suppose that Abraham did not have evidence, separate evidence, that this was the voice of God; nevertheless the voice itself was surely evidence. Had that voice been unintelligible, or gibberish, or inaudible, then it could not have even been the voice of God, or could not have even been understood. Had what the voice uttered not been in the imperative mood then it could not have been a command, and Abraham presumably had evidence that it was in the imperative mood; and so on.

Bouwsma may object that the voice is part of the human element in the story, not of the divine. Perhaps a condition of humanness is the capacity for whatever is humanly caused to provide evidence of itself. That would certainly be consistent, but then the divine element would not only be not human, it would be no-thing, something incapable of ever manifesting itself to Abraham or to anyone else. So there must be situations in which the human element is a necessary condition of the divine element being manifest, or being made apparent, or whatever. But if a condition *C* is a necessary condition for another condition *D*, then whatever is evidence for *C* is evidence for *D*.

Is it reasonable to interpret Bouwsma as offering a non-cognitivist account of religious belief? No. For him religious belief has a propositional structure, and the propositions have an objective referent; in the case of Abraham, the referent was God and what he commanded. There is therefore cognitive content to the belief. It is better to think of him as proposing the view that in some areas asking for evidence for one's belief is rather like making a category mistake.

So I conclude that Bouwsma has not made a persuasive case for the claim that trust in God is necessarily evidenceless, and therefore his claim cannot be used to support the conclusion that trusting God is unlike trusting anything or anyone else.

BARE PARTICULARITY

Finally, let us consider what I call the argument from bare particularity. It might be argued that what is special, and distinctive, about a personal relation is that there is about it an individuality or irreplacability; that what matters is that a personal relation is a relation between unique individuals. When a person loves his wife, the person he loves is not a sum of a set of properties, and were the person who is his wife to be secretly replaced by another woman who exactly replicated the person she replaced, the replacement would still lack the uniqueness of the person she replaced. It would thus make sense for A to say that, even though X is in all respects like Y except that X is numerically distinct from Y, it is rational to love Y and not X; that what makes the difference between X and Y is nothing that can be expressed in a property or set of properties that X possesses and Y lacks, or vice versa, but simply in the bare fact that X is X and not Y, or that Y is Y and not X.

Even if we assume that the idea of bare particularity, of an individual with no features, makes sense, the idea that trusting a person involves such particularity seems scarcely intelligible, much less rationally defensible. For if X and Y are different in no respect except that X is X and Y is Y, in virtue of what is X loved or loveable and Y not loved or loveable? The reason for X being loved and not Y, or vice versa, seems on such a view to be either irrationality or pure sentimentality, a love not grounded in anything about Y that is not also true of X, or vice versa. Even if it is accepted that love is irrational, what such irrationality means is not that love is based upon no evidence in the one loved, but that it is often based upon selective evidence, and that acting on that evidence may cut across a person's own best interests.

The same argument would apply to the possession of 'thisness'.[14] Let us suppose that a person cannot be accounted for solely in terms

[14] On 'thisness' see R. M. Adams, 'Primitive Thisness and Primitive Identity', *Journal of Philosophy*, 76 (1979), 5–26, and Richard Swinburne, *The Christian God* (Oxford, 1994), ch. 2.

of sets of general properties, including sets of relational properties, but that primitive 'thisness' is required for the individuation of any person. It makes no sense, it seems to me, even if 'thisness' is required for the full individuation of an individual, to suppose that given two individuals *A* and *B* with exactly the same monadic and relational properties, one might love *this* individual and not *that*. For in virtue of what would one love *A* rather than *B*? Just for being *this* individual?

One familiar and plausible principle of universalizability is that if some state of affairs *A* is in all respects like another state of affairs *B*, then it is incoherent to suppose that *A* is good and *B* not good. This is readily applicable to the case in hand. If *A* loves *B*, and *B* is in all respects like *C*, then it is unintelligible that *A* should love *B* and not *C*.

This account may be regarded as naive and unrealistic on the grounds that the reason why a person, say, loves his wife is not simply in virtue of a set of properties she possesses, but because of their joint history. No one else, no matter how many properties she shared with Jones's wife, could be his wife, since only his wife has participated in their joint history. This is a fair point. It is just the uniqueness of a person, of her being that person, that constitutes the relationship, and this cannot be replicated, since uniqueness cannot be replicated. This is true, but it is not a truth about persons only, but of anything, a machine or a non-human animal or a person, that has true individuality. An exact replica of my pen may be produced, but what is produced, though indistinguishable from it, is nevertheless not my pen, since it does not have the history of my pen.

For this reason I maintain that the argument from bare particularity or 'thisness', while defensible as an account of uniqueness, does not discriminate between uniqueness as it applies to persons and uniqueness as it applies to non-personal objects. And so I conclude that the difference thesis in general is not defensible.

CONCLUSION

My rejection of the four arguments for the difference thesis may each, either singly or together, contain some flaw. If the arguments are flawed, then what I think is needed by the proponents of the difference thesis in order for it to carry conviction is an account of trust which is not wholly univocal as between persons and things.

To illustrate, the English word 'know' might be said to have equivocal elements as between 'knowing how' and 'knowing that' or between 'knowing that' and 'being acquainted with'. Each of these pairs of expressions has an element in common which is in turn distinctive from other mental or cognitive expressions, and each has an element of difference. That they are not equivalent is seen from the fact that while it follows from 'A knows that S is ϕ' that it is possible that A is acquainted with S, from 'A is acquainted with S' it necessarily follows that A knows some true propositions about S. This gives us the element of difference. The element of similarity is given by the fact that from each of 'A knows that S is ϕ' and 'A knows S' it follows that there are propositions about S that A knows.

The challenge for the upholder of the difference thesis is to find uses of 'trust' with an analogical relationship between trusting people and trusting anything else. One possibility that we have touched upon earlier is the following: that if A trusts S then it is possible that S trusts A where S is a person, but not where S is something inanimate. There is no restriction upon the kinds of things that can be trusted, but only people can trust. This looks promising. But what about non-human animals? Some non-human animals can not only be trusted, they can trust as well; at least they can barring some Cartesian thesis about the mechanistic character of animal behaviour. Another possibility is that in the case of personal trust it is possible to trust a person without trusting him for anything in particular, but not so in the case of trusting things.

I do not think that either of these suggestions works. But maybe there is something like them that does work. What is certain is that something like this needs to work in order to establish the difference thesis on other than dogmatic or merely intuitive grounds.

8

Faith and Virtue

In this chapter I wish to apply the account of faith that I have been developing in earlier chapters—the evidential proportion view, as I have put it, according to which the strength of trust in an object of trust ought, other things being equal, to be proportioned to the strength of belief—to the problem of the relation between faith and action, or faith and virtue. We shall not consider the question of whether faith is itself a virtue, but rather some of the connections between faith and the moral virtues. One contemporary philosopher of religion who has paid considerable attention to this connection is Professor Richard Swinburne. And so I shall begin by first looking at relevant aspects of Professor Swinburne's discussion of faith in his book *Faith and Reason*. In particular, we shall focus on the question which runs like a central theme through his treatment of faith, 'May a scoundrel be a man of faith?' We shall conclude by making a further comparison between the view of faith favoured by Professor Swinburne and the evidential proportion view.

This question of the relation between faith and virtue may be understood as being about what was called, at the time of the Reformation and subsequently, the relation between faith and works. At the Reformation, answers to two such questions were at issue. The first concerned the nature of the connection between faith and works. Does faith include good works as part of its nature? The second question is, if anything, the more important: more important at the time of the Reformation, and more important subsequently, so it seems to me. This is the question of the respective roles of faith and good works in justification. Does faith alone justify, even though the faith which alone justifies is invariably accompanied by other graces? Or is it the possession of the grace of faith, and of the other graces that invariably accompany it, which justifies? On the answer to this question hangs the issue of whether or not justification is a forensic concept, of whether or not it has to do with legal and moral status, and hence of whether the righteousness that justifies is imputed or imparted righteousness.

There are those who have held in more recent times that this difference is purely semantic, and Professor Swinburne, whose views on faith we are about to explore, uses the ugly word 'logomachy' of this controversy. But it is far from being a strife about mere words. For the role that faith has in justification crucially affects what justification is. Happily, or unhappily, according to your point of view, we shall not be exploring this second question directly, for to do so would take us into the realms of Christian theology. We shall have more than enough on our plates in debating the less important question, the question of the connection between faith and works, the question of whether a man of faith can be a scoundrel.

Professor Swinburne has the capacity to stimulate fresh discussion on what at first sight may seem well-worn if not worn-out issues. He breathes new life into old bones, and I for one am glad that he does. In his discussion of Christian faith in *Faith and Reason* he claims, not surprisingly perhaps, that the answer to the question 'May a scoundrel be a man of faith?' is 'No'. But in the course of setting out his reasons for saying 'No' he has interesting and (to me at least) surprising things to say, both about the relation between faith and evidence, and about belief and trust, as well as about what he calls the Thomist, the Lutheran, and the Pragmatist views of faith.

One surprising thing is that in Professor Swinburne's opinion it is a criticism of both the Thomist and the Lutheran views of faith that they allow for something which, on his view, no satisfactory account of faith can allow for, that a scoundrel may be a man of faith. We shall not consider his criticisms of these views of faith in detail, but will instead examine what he has to say about the view of faith that he favours, what he calls the Pragmatist view of faith, the view already mentioned in an earlier chapter. For according to Swinburne it is only the Pragmatist view of what faith is which ensures that a man of faith cannot be a scoundrel. This view of faith may therefore act as a touchstone of the other views. Professor Swinburne says that the three views have a common structure and that the differences between them are mostly differences of emphasis,[1] though how these differences can amount to a mere matter of emphasis when the Thomist and the Lutheran views are allegedly defective in this central way is also surprising.

[1] Richard Swinburne, *Faith and Reason* (Oxford, 1981), 118.

We need to be clear what exactly lies behind the question, 'Can a scoundrel be a man of faith?' Swinburne is not asking, I take it, whether a man of faith can lapse into scurrility; nor is he asking, I think, whether a man may be a scoundrel at the time at which he becomes a man of faith. To each of these questions one imagines that he would answer 'Yes'. Rather he is concerned with the connectedness in principle between faith and well-motivated conduct.

I shall attempt to argue that Swinburne's view of faith and virtue, and the reasons he gives for it, reveal a paradox at the heart of his philosophical programme; or if not a paradox, then certainly a sharp divergence among his aims. I shall offer a tentative explanation of why this divergence occurs. And then in the final section of this chapter I shall contrast Swinburne's view of faith, which I earlier called the *evidential gap* view, with the view that I have been intermittently arguing for in this book, the *evidential proportion* view of faith. I shall in due course argue that there is no reason to think that the evidential proportion view of faith has the consequence that a scoundrel may be a man of faith.

So I shall agree (of course) with Swinburne that any view of faith that (in the sense already identified) permits scurrility by a man of faith is deficient. I shall accept this conclusion, but venture to disagree with some of his reasoning, and with the view of faith that underlies it.

FAITH AND BELIEF

We might approach the matter by considering once more the question, 'What, if anything, is involved in faith more than belief?' Swinburne sketches three different answers to the question. Thomas Aquinas's answer, according to Swinburne, is that—epistemically speaking—not much is needed for faith beyond belief. The devils and scoundrels are in the same epistemic boat as true pilgrims, at least until those pilgrims reach their celestial destination. They each have a belief based on revelation, a belief stronger than opinion but which does not amount to knowledge. Where they differ is in the source of their belief. The faith of the true pilgrims is belief that is uncoerced and freely chosen. While true faith is 'joined to the firm purpose of bringing about the works which the love of God ought properly to bring about',[2] according to Swinburne's account of Aquinas, there is a contingent connection between faith and the doing of God's work. The 'joining' may not in fact occur, and so the possibility that a man of faith might be a scoundrel remains.

According to Thomas the devils' belief, though genuine belief, is both coerced, and so not freely chosen, and also coupled with nefarious purposes. Is there likewise a contingent connection here? May the devils believe as they do but not act devilishly? Professor Swinburne does not address this question. For though the devils believe in God they do not trust him as their good. So on Thomas Aquinas's view it is only when faith is joined to or infused with love that scurrility becomes impossible; faith alone is not sufficient.

Martin Luther's answer to the question, according to Swinburne, is that the more which is needed for faith beyond belief is trust; the person of faith does not merely believe that there is a God (and believe certain other propositions about him)—she trusts him and commits herself to him. Such trust Professor Swinburne interprets as being action upon a certain assumption when there is some reason to doubt. We shall shortly be examining his reasons for taking this view. But he points out that a scoundrel may also act on a certain assumption, and in this sense also be a person of faith. He may trust in God but at the same time want what is in fact scurrilous. And so the Lutheran view cannot keep out the scoundrel, any more than the Thomistic view can. As Swinburne puts it,

The trouble with the Lutheran account of faith . . . is that it has in common with the Thomist account the feature that the perfect scoundrel may yet be a man of faith. For what you do when you act on an assumption depends on what your purposes are . . . A man may act on the assumption that God will do for him what he wants or needs, with purposes good or evil. Acting on that assumption, he may try to conquer the world, believing that God will help him in his task. Shall we call such a man a man of faith? Does he not trust God? Or the antinomian whom St. Paul attacks for suggesting that men should 'continue in sin, that grace may abound'. Does he not trust God, to see him right?[3]

He subjectively trusts God, but has a wrong conception of God.

---

[2] Ibid. 110.

[3] Ibid. 113. In his definition of faith and his subsequent criticisms of Aquinas's and Luther's views of faith Professor Swinburne does not take account of the fact that in the teaching of both the pre-Reformation and post-Reformation churches faith is always accompanied by other graces. For Aquinas, for example, the virtue of faith is inseparable from other virtues which together comprise that infused righteousness which justifies. For Luther and Calvin, justification is by faith alone, but the faith that

And so it emerges from these criticisms of Thomas Aquinas and Martin Luther that for Swinburne faith involves three elements—the propositional belief emphasized by Thomas (what Swinburne at more than one point calls 'theoretical' belief); trust, emphasized by Luther, understood as action upon an assumption; and having a good purpose. One can have belief in God and even trust him, and nevertheless be a scoundrel, because one is lacking in a good purpose. For one cannot both be a scoundrel about a matter and have a good purpose with regard to that matter. And so having a good purpose emerges as the crucial connection between faith and virtue because according to Swinburne there is a contingent connection between propositional belief, trust, and acting out of a good purpose, and only acting out of a good purpose is sufficient for virtuous action.

As we have just noted, as Swinburne understands the concept of trust it is an action and thus differs from belief, which is an effect. Trust is a case of acting on the assumption that p when there is some reason to doubt that p. Trust, that is, can occur in cases of evidential deficiency, and perhaps typically does occur there, though Swinburne recognizes that one may put one's trust in what one believes to be almost certain as well as what one believes to be somewhat unlikely. But it is not possible to place one's trust in what one is completely certain about, and the less certain one is, the more room there is for trust.

However, the focus of attention in *Faith and Reason* is on faith as trust in a situation of weak belief and even where there is little or no belief. In such cases to trust, that is, to act on the assumption that p, is to act as if p were more certain than it is. So trust makes up for evidential deficiency; the subjective certainty of faith, and the connection between faith and action, is stronger than the evidence alone warrants. In the case of religious trust, trust in God, in so far as such trust goes beyond the evidence it anticipates the fullness of evidence that (it is believed) the beatific vision will bring. What is significant for Swinburne is that where little or no belief exists, but trust does, then trust is acting *as if* one believed. Swinburne illustrates these claims about trust as follows:

I may trust a friend by lending a valuable to him when he has previously proved careless with valuables. I act on the assumption that he will do what

alone justifies is never on its own. See Aquinas, *Summa Theologiae*, IaIIae. 1–7; Calvin, *Institutes of the Christian Religion*, III. xiv.

he knows that I want . . . where the evidence gives some reason for supposing that he will not, and where there are bad consequences . . . if he does not.[4]

So typically and centrally trust is acting on the assumption that
another person will do as I want when I have good reason to doubt
this. And religious trust is such trust where the object of trust is God.

A PARADOX?

Perhaps there are cases of trust which occur in the absence of evidence, but to decouple trust and belief in the systematic way that
Swinburne does leads to the following paradoxical situation. Take
two people *A* and *B* and a proposition *p*, and suppose that *A* has evidence for *p* which renders *p* slightly more probable than not-*p* for
him, while *B* has evidence that makes *p* highly probable for him.
Each may behave in a similar way with respect to the truth expressed
by *p*, but on Professor Swinburne's account one of these may be a
man of considerable faith, acting on an assumption with a good purpose, while the other will have a strong belief, acting as a consequence of possessing good evidence, but may have only little faith.
As Swinburne puts it, to trust is 'to do those actions which you would
do if you believed the stated assumption strongly'.[5] So someone who
believes the assumption strongly, and reasonably, i.e. has good evidence for it, is badly placed to exercise trust, and so to possess and
exercise faith. Thus it appears that the better grounded the belief, or
for that matter the better grounded the unbelief, the less scope there
is for faith. Strong belief or unbelief expel faith, or at least they considerably reduce the opportunities for its exercise.

One might suppose that, whatever its difficulties, such a view is at
least theologically sound; for does not St Paul imply that while faith
and hope are temporary, love is eternal? Perhaps he does. But it does
not necessarily follow from this that there is no trust in a situation
where faith is turned to sight. Perhaps the saints made perfect, who
know and love God completely, also for that very reason trust him
completely. What may be temporary, on this interpretation of St
Paul, is not trust but belief, which is replaced by knowledge in the life
to come.

---

[4] Swinburne, *Faith and Reason*, 111.   [5] Ibid. 112.

However this may be, it is here, at the point where faith is decoupled from belief, that what appears to be an interesting conflict of aims in Professor Swinburne's work as a philosopher of religion comes into view. For on the one hand he wishes, in many of his writings, vigorously (and rigorously) to prosecute the question of whether or not there is good evidence that God exists, and to go to considerable pains to assemble that evidence. As is well known, Professor Swinburne takes the view that for belief in God's existence to be reasonable there must be more evidence for that proposition than for its negation. And the more evidence that can be assembled for the truth of the proposition, the better. This is the burden of his book *The Existence of God*, for example.

So in order to be reasonable in his believing a person must strive to ensure that there is more evidence for the truth of the proposition that he believes than for some alternative proposition. He must have as one of his intellectual aims the grounding of belief in evidence as firmly as he can. According to Swinburne such belief is not free, for belief is not voluntary. He is a good Humean at this point; belief is that state of mind which is constrained by what that mind takes to be good evidence. Choosing to believe is incoherent. And the intellectually responsible person must be as sure as he can be that what he takes to be good evidence is in fact good evidence, and he must tie his belief as firmly as he can to the evidence; his belief must be *on* the evidence.

But such a view of belief has interesting and perhaps disturbing consequences for faith. According to Swinburne the better grounded a belief, the less free is that belief. Such belief is not so much an action as an effect, it is the mind being involuntarily impressed by what it takes to be evidence. So believing is not an action, and *a fortiori* it cannot be morally assessed as an action. It makes no sense to ask whether belief is meritorious or not, for example. A person can neither be praised for believing, nor blamed for not believing, though she may be praised or blamed for the way in which she approaches matters which are necessary conditions for believing, for example, for her attitude to the correct assessment of evidence. So, in the case of someone who has good evidence for *p*, and who accordingly believes strongly that *p*, there is less scope for free trust in what *p* expresses than where belief is less strongly grounded. For trust, according to Swinburne, goes beyond the evidence; it operates where there is good reason to doubt. And, because Swinburne links the exercise of trust and possession of merit in such a situation, there is less scope for merit where belief is well grounded.[6] To the extent that the existence of God is evidentially established it is more reasonable to believe that he exists than not, but for that very reason there is less opportunity for faith in him, for trust. Merit comes only from trust, but trust can only occur when there is evidential deficiency. On Professor Swinburne's view it would seem that as the God of the philosophers, the God of reasonable belief, enters by the front door, the God of Abraham, Isaac, and Jacob, the God who is trusted, is forced to leave by the rear exit!

So if you want to exercise trust in God, and to gain merit by its exercise, as Swinburne claims that you will, you had better not read Swinburne's *The Existence of God* and you most certainly ought not to let yourself be persuaded by strong grounds to believe in God's existence or be similarly persuaded about any other proposition about God. For to the extent that you have good grounds for a belief about God you at the same time reduce the opportunities for trusting God, for acting on an assumption while having a good purpose, and so you reduce the opportunities for faith in God, and so lessen your chances of gaining merit by exercising such faith. Faith may never be eliminated altogether, because there may always be propositions about God which one has poor grounds for and yet wishes to exercise trust in; nevertheless the scope for faith will be considerably reduced. And the project of the reasonable man, to the extent that it is successful, may knowingly reduce the opportunities that he has for exercising faith.

But, it may perhaps be replied, the argument rests upon a confusion. While belief is involuntary, taking steps to acquire and lose beliefs is a voluntary activity, and so may be meritorious. But then the certain merit to be gained from an investigation into God's existence which includes carefully reading *The Existence of God* has to be weighed against the prospect of being convinced by its arguments and so of reducing the opportunities for the exercise of meritorious faith in the future. So perhaps one has to balance the merit of carefully reading *The Existence of God* against the merit of not reading it.

One might also argue that one can be certain that God exists and be quite uncertain of some of God's properties and that trusting in God is in respect of those matters about God that one is uncertain of.

---

[6] See Richard Swinburne, *The Existence of God* (Oxford, 1979), 244.

This is undoubtedly a possibility, though certainty of God's existence cannot be coupled with agnosticism about all his properties, presumably. And it is as important to investigate the character of God as it is to investigate his existence. Once one acquires beliefs about his character the opportunities for trust in God are further reduced.

Perhaps indeed one has an *obligation* to investigate as thoroughly as one can the question of whether God exists. If in this situation one does investigate the question, then one fulfils this obligation, and so (presumably) gains merit. But in fulfilling this obligation, and so gaining merit, one lessens the chances of living a life of faith, and so of gaining merit by such a life. So perhaps one has to balance the merit arising from responsibly investigating the grounds of one's faith against the merit to be gained from exercising that faith in an unreflective way and so of exercising trust. Such are the problems of meritology.

We have already noted that Swinburne tends to decouple trust and belief, and to favour the view that the strength of one's trust is inversely proportional to the strength of one's belief. So strongly and clearly does Swinburne hold to the idea that trusting is an action that (as we noted in Chapter 6) he is able to contemplate with surprising equanimity the idea that there is a form of faith, Pragmatist faith,[7] according to which a person may act as if God exists without having any belief that he does and, possessing good will, free himself from scurrility and so gain merit. If Swinburne is consistent then he must also maintain that such a view holds out the prospect of the greatest scope for trust, and so of the greatest degree of merit in trusting. On such a view faith has an intentional object, but that object need not be God in order for the faith to be genuine. If I believe that there is a God then the intentional object of my belief is 'that there is a God', whereas if I believe that it is possible that there is a God the intentional object of my belief is 'that it is possible there is a God'. Pragmatist faith is compatible with the belief that there just possibly may be a God. Such faith can hardly be said to be faith in God. On such a view God's existence is not impossible, but neither is it more probable than not. Typically, for the Pragmatist view of faith it is more probable than not that God does not exist. To have faith in such circumstances is to act on the assumption that there is such a God, rather like the would-be believer in Pascal's Wager. As Swinburne puts it,

[7] Swinburne, *Faith and Reason*, 115.

it is natural enough to develop this third view of faith [i.e. the Pragmatist view] according to which the belief-that is irrelevant, the acting-as-if is what matters. After all belief is a passive state; merit belongs only to actions.[8]

Pragmatist faith emphasizes, perhaps places exclusive emphasis upon, acting-as-if, and acting-as-if is acting on the assumption that *p* with a good purpose, when there is some reason, but not a good reason, for thinking that *p* is true. So if, after having read and pondered Swinburne's *The Existence of God*, you still have grave doubts about whether God exists, you ought not to despair of faith; you may have faith, Pragmatist faith, provided that God's existence remains a possibility for you. To ensure that you have such faith you need to be able to act with a good purpose, to resolve not to be a scoundrel and to act accordingly. Indeed, in these circumstances you have the greatest scope for faith. And so those who, epistemologically speaking, are first shall, fiducially speaking, be last; and the last shall be first. The evidentially hungry shall be filled, while the evidentially rich shall be sent empty away.

As we have noted, Swinburne suggests that in order to save its rationality such a view needs the belief that there is some non-zero possibility less than 0.5 that there is a God; that is, that there is some likelihood that there is a God but that it is more likely that there is not. Whether this can be belief as he elsewhere understands it is doubtful, for in *Faith and Reason* Swinburne appears to define belief in terms of what a person takes to be more probable than not.[9] Perhaps what he means at this point is that for the Pragmatist believer it is more probable than not that it is possible there is a God. Such a person may without doubt be trustful, but if there is more evidence that favours the view that God will not keep his promises than that he will, perhaps because it is likely that he does not exist, ought not one to that extent to withhold one's trust? At best, such a person would have a *motive* for having faith, but not a *reason* for having it.

Indeed, it would be better to characterize such an attitude not as Pragmatist faith, but as hope. Both religious trust and hope are oriented towards the future, but hope can more intelligibly and plausibly be exercised in the absence of very much evidence. Without any evidence, certainly without a balance of evidence in favour of *p*, it

---

[8] Ibid. 116.

[9] For further discussion of Swinburne's view of belief see William P. Alston, 'Swinburne on Faith and Belief', in Alan G. Padgett (ed.), *Reason and the Christian Religion* (Oxford, 1994).

makes perfect sense that a person will nevertheless hope that what p describes will come to pass.

So why is it at all appropriate to say that such people have faith? Surely they are hopers rather than believers? Swinburne's argument is that a person may put his trust in something which, on balance, he does not believe to exist.[10] But this does not seem at all plausible. A person may trust A and A not exist; a case of mistakenly directed belief. But how could he trust A while not at all believing that A exists or while having the belief that it is merely possible that A exists? 'I trust God but I do not believe that he exists' looks like a paradox of belief to rival G. E. Moore's; and 'I trust God and I believe that it's merely possible that he exists' is scarcely less paradoxical.

Swinburne believes that he detects a convergence between the Thomist, the Lutheran, and the Pragmatist views of faith;[11] for as he sees it, each thinks of faith as involving three elements: belief-that, a good character expressed in good actions, and trust. Each view has the same ingredients, but different proportions of each, though it still remains that the Thomist and the Lutheran views allow that a man of faith may be a scoundrel, whereas the Pragmatist view does not. I shall not comment further on either the historical accuracy or the plausibility of this claim, but rather focus for the remainder of this chapter on the account of trust which Swinburne reckons to be common to all three views.

TRUST

From a romantic, counter-cultural, and generally Kierkegaardian point of view there is, no doubt, much to be said for the account of trust that underlies Swinburne's Pragmatist view of faith, what we have called the evidential deficiency view of trust. And besides, there are often good reasons why a person may trust some person or thing in the absence of evidence for, and even in the presence of evidence against, the trustworthiness of what is trusted. Even the evidential proportion view of faith that we are defending need not be understood so rigidly that faith cannot be sustained in the face of temporary deficiencies of evidence or the sudden appearing of

---

[10] Swinburne, *Faith and Reason*, 167.   [11] Ibid. 117 f.

counter-evidence. There may arise good inductive evidence to show that temporary deficiencies of evidence can soon be replenished. A principle of tenacity may be rational provided that one is not indefinitely tenacious in the face of ever-mounting counter-evidence.

Another good reason for trusting even in the absence of evidence has to do with the value placed upon the object of trust. Perhaps a father ought to continue to trust that the police will find his boy alive even while travelling to identify a body. Perhaps someone seriously ill with cancer ought to believe that he will recover. But if the role of the philosopher of religion is not only to record the diverse evidential shapes that trust may take, but also to recommend a conception of trust by argument, is there much to be said on epistemological grounds for a view of trust which is evidentially indistinguishable from foolhardiness? Perhaps doubting Thomas ought to have trusted when he could not see, but ought he still to have trusted had he possessed much less evidence than he did in fact possess?

Still, I do not wish to say that Swinburne's account of trust, the *evidential gap* view as I have called it, is not a defensible account of trust. Clearly if an evidential element and a purposive element are each necessary elements for any account of trust, there is room for differences of view about the respective importance to be attached to evidence and purpose. There will be cases where there is little evidence and great strength of purpose, and cases where there is much evidence but where purpose is weak. These may each be cases of trust. Where the mix of evidence and purpose becomes a little hard to swallow is where the belief is no stronger than belief in the bare possibility that God exists.

It seems much more reasonable to formulate an account of faith which *proportions* the strength of trust to the strength of belief through all the ranges of belief, from belief that it is just on balance more likely than not that God exists upwards to full certainty; the proportion view of belief and trust, as I have called it. This has the consequence of making the Pragmatist view of faith (at best) a case of very weak belief, warranting very weak trust, but then that is precisely what it seems to be.

As we have noted, Swinburne maintains that trusting is an action whereas believing is not, and in a way this can hardly be disputed. But is trust in God a case of a morally good action, perhaps the paradigm case of such an action, as he maintains, and as he needs to maintain if he is to link faith and merit as robustly as he does? Is there not a critical moral difference between trust as the basis of the action of doing something and trust as the basis for receiving something? And is not the basic religious stance of trustfulness, at least in Christianity, that of one who trusts he will receive, rather than trusting as the basis of doing something and so of gaining merit thereby? And even were Swinburne to be right both about trust being an action, and about it being a meritorious action, would it, as such an action, be intelligible in the absence of a measure of confidence that the one who is being trusted exists? May a person meritoriously act by trusting in God when he does not believe that there is a God, though he believes there may be? He may, under these circumstances, trust *that there is a God* (which is hardly the same thing as trusting God). Accordingly he may act with a good purpose, in fulfilment of what he takes to be the will of God, if he exists, though he could hardly think that his action was meritorious in the sight of God.

Why does Swinburne focus his attention upon the evidential gap view of trust and upon trust as an action, views which stress non-evidential and non-rational elements? The answer is not altogether clear. One reason for focusing upon trust as an action may be that, because of his account of belief, he cannot make trust a matter of irrational belief. For as we have already noted, on his view of belief it is impossible for someone to believe what he does not, on the balance of probabilities, believe to be more likely than not. Because Swinburne takes this view and wishes to think of trust as a moral action he cannot think of belief as essential to it.

A more likely reason for Swinburne emphasizing the evidential gap between evidence and trust appears to be that he wishes to preserve a place for human freedom in the exercise of trust, because he has theological reasons for keeping a place for merit in faith. We have already noted that Swinburne is a strong involuntarist as regards belief,[12] holding that in the short term we cannot help having the beliefs we do have. Because of his views on the centrality of merit in religion Swinburne must thus maintain that there is a voluntaristic something more to transform belief into faith, and so to make it meritorious. And this voluntaristic something more is an action which ventures beyond belief by acting as if the belief had a stronger evidential warrant than it has. It may even detach itself from belief altogether. Ignorance may be bliss, but is it not stretching things to suppose that it is also the source of religious virtue?

[12] See especially Ibid. ch. 1.

Irrespective of whether or not faith is meritorious it seems on the whole desirable that it should, in its typical expressions, be voluntary, unclear though that term often is. (Yet one should exercise caution here; in the stories that we possess of his conversion, one does not gain the impression that the faith of Saul of Tarsus was first exercised voluntarily. It seems to have been wrung from him.) But even if one shares the view that faith is typically voluntary, whatever precisely this means, one does not have to resort to irrational or ungrounded expressions of trust to secure voluntariness. It is possible for trust of a certain strength to be intellectually coerced to that degree by the evidence and so, in an important sense, for trust not to be free. But though it is coerced it may be willingly coerced; that is, the one who trusts may come to welcome the inevitability of his belief, perhaps as Saul of Tarsus came to. In some cases the proposition which the evidence favours may be shocking and unwelcome; but in other cases it may be the fulfilment of all a person's hopes.

Even if one shares Swinburne's anxieties about the need to secure merit through voluntariness, his way of ensuring such voluntariness has an odd look to it. The voluntariness is secured by the fact that the evidence which ensures the belief does not also ensure the action. The action is ensured by the purpose. Whatever the source of the purpose, it does not arise solely or mainly from the evidence for the truth of a proposition on which the purpose is based. Purpose may outrun belief, and may run in the absence of belief. Such purposing is from the self, and so is a metaphysically free act, and *a fortiori* uncoerced.

Even if one is attracted to such indeterminism, as I am not, this seems to be an odd way of securing voluntariness in the case of religious faith. For there is in any case a contingent connection between beliefs about matters of fact and purposes, as is shown by the fact that opposite purposes may exist in different people who share beliefs. Although religion may not be the slave of the passions, it may be passionate; and while its passions may not be caused by evidence, they may be proportioned and conditioned by it. In other words, the voluntariness which Swinburne desires to preserve for faith could be secured with less loss to rationality than in his scheme in *Faith and Reason*.

The final reason which Swinburne may have for favouring the evidential gap view of trust, and his belief that trust is an action, has to do with some of those whom he thinks it is appropriate to call men and women of faith. He holds[13] that there are people who believe that it is good to pursue the right religious goals (e.g. the vision of God in heaven) and who at the same time lack the belief that they will get there, because they lack the belief in God, though they have other beliefs.

The man of Pragmatist faith need not believe that there is a God, but he must have certain other beliefs. He has to have moral beliefs . . . beliefs about his long-term well-being . . . and beliefs about the best route to attain that well-being. And he needs the belief that there is some (maybe small) finite probability that there is a God.[14]

As we have seen, the belief that the probability that there is a God is greater than zero may nevertheless entail the belief that probably God does not exist. Nevertheless, according to Professor Swinburne, provided that such a disbeliever has certain moral beliefs it is reasonable to suppose that he has faith, because such people have, in these circumstances, the right stance towards God. They are men and women of good will, having a good purpose. So they have the essence of trust, even though they may lack its accidents. But such a view seems not to ally faith and good will, but to confuse the two.

THE EVIDENTIAL PROPORTION VIEW OF FAITH

Is there a more plausible view of faith than the evidential gap view which lies at the heart of Swinburne's account of faith? In a sense, of course, any view of faith will be evidentially gappy. For even the evidence that ensures knowledge is never as much evidence as there might be. There is always a gap between the evidence which justifies a belief and the evidence which entails the truth of the proposition that is believed, a gap which the philosophical sceptic notoriously exploits. Furthermore, if faith involves belief but not knowledge the gap may be considerable. Nevertheless, I wish to argue, both knowledge possessed at present and the knowledge of the beatific vision will each be compatible with trust in the propositions known. For trust is not primarily an epistemological notion, nor does it typically function only where there is evidential deficiency.

---

[13] Ibid. 117 f.   [14] Ibid. 117.

So, short of incorrigibility there may be all the evidence for a particular proposition that it is reasonable to have, and such evidence might amount to good evidence. I shall argue that even in such circumstances of evidential plenitude the possibility of, and the need for, trust (understood not as acting-as-if but as reliance upon the truth of what is believed and so upon the one who utters or in other ways manifests what he believes) does not diminish; and moreover that trust may be appropriate only in such circumstances.

Further, even where the evidence is not as good as it could be, there is a significant difference between trust making up for evidential deficiency and trust being proportioned to belief to the degree warranted by the available evidence. In both cases trust is fiducial, it is the fiducial element of faith, but on the evidential deficiency view there is no good reason for the trust having the strength that it has, whereas on the proportion view the good reason is simply the degree of subjective evidence that the belief is supported by. On the alternative view of trust that I am proposing trust ought to be proportioned to the strength of the corresponding belief. Anything less than this, and faith is weaker than it ought to be; anything more, and faith becomes hard to distinguish from credulity and foolhardiness. On this view what distinguishes trust from mere belief is not that it makes up for evidential deficiency but that it is an act of reliance upon the one whom, it is believed, can meet some need or fulfil some goal.

Let us consider a simple illustration. A person may trust a footbridge not because he has some reason to doubt that it will bear his weight (the evidential deficiency view of trust), but precisely because he has reason not to doubt that it alone can get him to the other side of the ravine. On such a view trust in the bridge is compatible with and exercised in a situation of evidential plenitude; it is not a makeweight for evidential deficiency. Alternatively a person may trust the footbridge when, although he has some reason to doubt its strength, it matters a great deal to him to get to the other side. Here it is the purpose to get across, the agent's desire to achieve his goal of attaining the other side of the ravine, that produces the trust; nevertheless, even in this situation, the strength of the trust ought to be affected by the strength of the evidence for the belief on which the trust is based.

Is this a counter-example to what I have been arguing for, the proportional view of belief to evidence, and trust to belief? Not really.

Other things being equal, the degree of trust ought to be proportioned to the degree of belief. But other things may not be equal, particularly in the short term, and so the degree of trust may be a function not only of the degree of belief but of the strength of desire. What is true of things is true of persons. A man may be said to trust his wife when he has no reason to think that she will be unfaithful. Alternatively he may trust his wife when he has reason to doubt her faithfulness but when he very much wants her to remain his wife. Where there is no reason to doubt, the trust, though real, may not disclose itself in an awareness of trust, but may be highly dispositional, like the fact that we each of us now trust that the surface of the Earth will bear our weight. Swinburne's view appears to carry with it the paradoxical consequence that the more certain a man is of his wife's faithfulness the less he trusts her!

So there are cases of trust which depend upon belief and are proportioned to the evidential strength or weakness of the belief and these cases seem to be less paradoxical than Swinburne's view. If we put to one side problems raised by weakness of will we may even say: weak belief, weak trust; strong belief, strong trust. To parody David Hume, on this view a wise man proportions his trust to his belief.

But may not a person, on occasion, on account of the strength of his purposes and desires, and in the face of unexpected counter-evidence, trust in a tenacious, Job-like way beyond what is warranted by the present evidence on which his belief is based? Yes he may, but it is not of the *bene esse* of trust to do so. Though cases of such trust may be overall rational because it may be rational to maintain one's purposes in a situation in which there is little evidence to support them, it may not be epistemically rational to do so. It is sometimes said that cases like that of Abraham are instances of faith being exercised in spite of total evidence against. But this does not seem plausible. After all, Abraham believed that God had called him and had grounds for this belief. However, there are additional complications here. As we noted earlier, over a period of time a person may come to have good inductive evidence that the appearing of counter-evidence to a belief he holds is temporary. On this view it would be reasonable to continue to believe even in the face of counter-evidence. Perhaps Abraham was sometimes in this position.

So on the proportional view of faith and evidence, evidence to a degree is what is epistemically sufficient for faith to that degree, but other, non-epistemic factors are also necessary, and one of those factors is the agent's purpose to attain what he believes upon evidence to be true. He does not believe because he wants to believe, but he believes because of the evidence and his belief is in an important sense voluntary, in the sense that he wants what he believes. According to the Apostle James the devils believe. But they do not want the truth that their evidence points to, and so may not be said to trust God for anything.

One further advantage which the evidential proportion view of belief and faith possesses is that it enables one to provide a clear account of degrees of trust. On this view the degree to which a person may trust another is no more or less difficult to grasp than the idea of the degree of his belief, since it is directly related to it. In those cases where it goes beyond the evidence, it might be possible to defend the rationality of faith on the grounds that it is correlated both with the evidence and the good that is desired. Since on Swinburne's view the degree of trust is a function of two completely independently operating factors, the degree of belief and the strength of purpose, *A* may trust *B* more than *C* does even though *A* and *C* are in the same epistemic boat and *A*'s greater trust is due solely to the greater strength of *A*'s purpose.

But does the evidential proportion view do justice to what may be regarded as one of the distinctive and essential features of faith, and one that is often given great prominence, its riskiness? It would seem so; the riskiness of faith, where it is risky, attaches not to the trust per se, but to the degree of belief. The different degrees of trust correspond to the different degrees of belief in the case of those who exercise faith. Some degree of trust is compatible with some degree of doubt, and if one trusts at the same time as one entertains doubts one is knowingly taking a risk. But risk may also be involved in so far as the believer takes into account not only the grounds of his belief, but his desire for what his belief expresses. His desire may be so great as to justify action, the action of trusting God, even when the grounds for the belief are weak.

Because of the evidential gap between the evidence on which faith is based, and the truth of what is believed, all faith involves some risk, since only incorrigible knowledge totally excludes epistemic risk. And though knowledge that is less than incorrigible does not exclude belief, at least on most modern analyses of knowledge, all that this shows is that while faith and belief are distinct, they are not totally distinct. Or, alternatively, it shows that knowledge and trust are not incompatible. When, to use St Paul's language, the believer sees face to face, God will not cease to be trusted.

Finally, where does the scoundrel fit in on the view of belief, trust, and evidence that I have been arguing is to be preferred to Swinburne's account? We began by noting Swinburne's concern about the need to relate faith and works. He excludes the possibility of a scoundrel being a man of faith not by arguing that belief and trust are together sufficient for such exclusion but by requiring that belief and trust (i.e. acting on an assumption) must be conjoined with a good purpose, and by even suggesting, in his account of Pragmatist faith, that the good purpose is the dominant element in faith.

On the alternative account that I am offering, the proportional view of faith and evidence, a good purpose is not conceptually distinct from true faith. The scoundrel may at best exemplify only one of the two elements of faith. He may be aware of the proposition p in question, and may regard it as true, assenting to it. But due to his scurrility, the scoundrel does not want for himself what p promises. For instance he may want God to help him to conquer the world, or to rifle the till, but have no warrant for believing that God will help him to do such things. He may be offered the kingdom of God, but refuse it. On the proportional view trust does not make up the evidential lack of belief, it presupposes a certain want or need of the believer's and some evidentially based confidence that the want will be met by the object of faith. Because the scoundrel does not have the relevant want or need, but possesses some incompatible need, he cannot be a true believer.

The trust itself, what the believer is prepared to trust God for, either is or reveals a moral disposition of a certain sort or range. That disposition is revealed in the sort of things that one is prepared to trust God for under certain descriptions. If you trust God because you believe that he will bring you health and wealth and this is all you want, the trust reveals a different schedule of values from trusting God because you believe that he will forgive your sins and this is what you want.

I have argued that the evidential proportion view of faith both avoids certain paradoxes generated by Richard Swinburne's account, and can well account for the central features of Christian faith. In faith, over the long term, belief ought to be proportioned to evidence, and desire to belief. But in the short term, and where desire is stronger than belief, it may nevertheless be rational to have a belief whose strength is greater than present evidence warrants.

9

Faith and Self-reflection

In the first chapter I maintained that the philosophy of religion is best conducted in relation not to some abstract or minimalist conception of 'religion', but in relation to the doctrines and concerns of particular religions. I have tried to follow my own advice in looking at the relation between faith in the Christian tradition in its fiducial and evidential aspects, and at the relation of faith to virtue. I have argued that one of the elements in religious faith as opposed to mere belief is that the object of religious faith has an importance that is different from mere theoretical importance. Religious faith is not merely a matter of thin belief, where purely theoretical interests and constraints apply, but of thick belief, involving issues of practical moment. There is a link between faith and virtue, but that link is not that faith is itself a meritorious virtue, but that it is exercised in the expression of certain characteristic needs and desires which provide a conceptual connection between religious faith and the commitment to moral endeavour.

So part of the structure of faith, including religious faith, is not simply that one who has faith has good evidence for what is trusted in, but also that he has a set of beliefs about what is desirable for himself. So faith involves two sorts of beliefs: beliefs about oneself, and beliefs about things other than oneself. In this final chapter I shall concentrate attention on one particular belief about oneself, namely on the belief that I am myself a believer. This is not a belief about what I want, but a belief about what is believed to be true of me; that is, it is a second-order belief, a belief about a belief.

FAITH AND ASSURANCE

Inside the front cover of my second-hand copy of the Cambridge theologian John Oman's book *Grace and Personality* a previous owner has pasted a short newspaper cutting with these words:

'A Methodist', Jones said, 'knows he's got religion, but he's afraid he'll lose it. A Presbyterian knows he can't lose it, but he's afraid he hasn't got it.'

For countless people the question of the relation between faith and evidence is not the question that has preoccupied us in earlier chapters, the question of whether or not there is enough evidence—call it objective evidence—to warrant what I earlier called thin belief in God, belief in God which is formed under constraints which are wholly theoretical in character. Nor is it even the question of whether thick belief is warranted. Such people take it for granted that there is enough evidence to warrant thick belief.

Rather, what preoccupies them is the question of whether or not they possess enough evidence—call it subjective evidence—to warrant the belief that they are themselves believers. That is, they are concerned with belief as a practical issue, held not only under the constraints of rationality and empirical evidence, but also of time and of value. And they are concerned, naturally enough, to establish that they themselves have such faith. For it is one of the prevailing characteristics of the two senses of belief that I earlier distinguished that, while having belief in the thin sense has been held not to matter very much, except to academic philosophers of religion, having thick belief has been held to matter a great deal. Much—in the history of Christian thought and practice, for example—has turned on the question of whether or not a person is a thick believer. And so the question of whether one is entitled to believe that one is a thick believer has been, and for countless people still is, a pressing question.

However, the investigation of this subjective evidence may itself be a matter either of theoretical or practical enquiry, leading to appropriate thin or thick beliefs about it. Sometimes, so it seems to me, religious perplexity of a certain kind has been due to a confusion of the two. Thus the excessive introspectionism which was characteristic of English Puritanism, and of certain kinds of pietism, a religious state of mind in which men and women continually search their inner states for sure signs of divine grace, might plausibly be explained as being due to an insistence on theoretical levels of certitude in what is a non-theoretical situation. Some of this introspectionism—though not introspection per se—undoubtedly has elements of philosophical scepticism about it. Some have been so convinced of their own unworthiness in the sight of God that it has seemed to them as if no standard of subjective evidence, or almost no standard, would be sufficiently high to provide enough evidence that God has been gracious to them in granting them the grace of faith. The question can never be satisfactorily settled for them because the standard of evidence that they demand is so exalted; hence the gnawing anxiety and even despair that such introspection often produces.

There is a wide range of conditions which have counted and do count in the minds of philosophers and others that would justify a belief that there is a God in the thin sense; these all have to do with sufficient evidence, or with its absence, for the proposition that there is a God. In the case of thick belief there is similarly a wide range of conditions for genuineness, but some of these conditions have to do not with whether there are grounds for believing that God exists, but with whether, in addition to such belief, a person has evidence that he genuinely trusts God.

Given that evidence of thick belief partly depends upon subjective evidence, upon the evidence of a person's own subjective states, his beliefs about himself, including what he does or intends to do, there is a clear logical difference between having sufficient evidence to warrant the trust and having sufficient evidence that one is actually trusting. One may have evidence that is sufficient for reasonable belief and then, in addition, sufficient evidence that one actually has such belief. For the evidence on the basis of which a person trusts, even if that evidence is self-evidence, does not itself contain the evidence of that person trusting, but that conclusion must be a further inference requiring other grounds.

A person's trust in *A*, whether this is a component of religious or non-religious faith, can never be equivalent to or contain the second-order belief that a person trusts in *A*. For a person does not have grounds for believing that he trusts God, even though he may in fact do so, unless he has whatever may be considered to be the appropriate subjective evidence that he does so. It is not sufficient merely to believe that one trusts, for it is notorious that a person may mistakenly think that he trusts another when he does not, and vice versa.

There is more to trusting than believing that some object of attention is trustworthy, and more to knowing or believing that one trusts than the mere fact of trusting. Apart from his recognition of the evidence of such trust, which includes subjective evidence, there is no warrant for a person to conclude that he trusts. It may be true that he trusts, but he has no warrant for believing that he does so without awareness of this evidence.

In saying that there is a logical distinction between evidence that warrants a first-order belief and evidence that warrants a second-order belief it does not follow that there is necessarily a temporal distinction between the two. A person may believe and then, later, believe that he believes. But he may not; the two states, though logically distinct, may be fused together in time, and there be no time when that person reasonably believed but did not reasonably believe that he believed.

No doubt one of the reasons for the importance attached to visions, voices, or dreams by a certain kind of religious adherent is that such phenomena are believed to provide direct evidence to a person that he, that person, is a true believer; for in the vision or dream, or by the voice, he may be addressed by name, or seem to be looked at and talked to in unmistakable fashion. This is particularly so if the religion in question instructs its adherents to wait for the vision, or to seek the dream. Such evidence has often been said by religious sceptics to be fraudulent, or to be weak evidence of the 'ten leaky buckets' variety. But it strikes me that evidence of this general sort can be fairly good evidence. If your bird-spotting friend tells you that if you wait by the tree you will see a flycatcher, and you wait, and you see the flycatcher, is this not reasonable evidence that your friend is a genuinely good bird watcher?

Similarly with religion; if your religion tells you that under certain circumstances you will have an assuring voice or vision, and in these circumstances you do, this seems prima facie good evidence for the genuineness of the religion, and of your rational entitlement to be assured by the vision or voice. No doubt there are kinds of situation in which a dream or a vision might be induced in religiously inappropriate ways, e.g. by eating a heavy meal or by imbibing a hallucinogenic substance. But developed religions usually are able to cater for such eventualities.

So our concern in this chapter is not so much with faith as with the personal assurance of faith, with the belief that a person has that he has faith, and with some of the logical and philosophical issues that this idea raises.

THE CONDITIONS OF ASSURANCE

One famous expression of the assurance of faith in this sense can be found in John Wesley's well-known words, to which I wish to give some attention in what follows. Wesley described an experience he had at a religious meeting in Aldersgate as follows:

About a quarter before nine [in the evening], while he [one of the Moravian Brethren] was describing the change which God works in the heart through faith in Christ, I felt my heart strangely warmed. I felt I did trust in Christ; Christ, alone for salvation; and an assurance was given me that he had taken away *my* sins, even *mine*, and saved *me* from the law of sin and death.[1]

Wesley here makes a distinction between faith or trust in Christ to take away his sins, a trust which no doubt involved belief, and the recognition of this fact, a recognition that also involved certain beliefs, for example the belief that Christ had taken away his sins, a recognition which he calls an 'assurance'. He trusted Christ alone for salvation, and it seems from what he writes that he was almost immediately assured that he did indeed so trust Christ, and that his sins were indeed forgiven. So in the assurance of faith (at least as Wesley understood it) the emphasis does not lie on the objective grounds that a person may have for reasonably believing the truths of the Christian faith, the sort of question that preoccupies much modern debate about the relation between faith and reason, and has preoccupied us in earlier chapters, but with the personal, subjective grounds that someone may have for believing that he himself is a believer, and so in a position to enjoy whatever benefits faith may yield. In undertaking this enquiry the objective grounds for the reasonableness of faith are taken for granted.

Behind this famous remark of Wesley's lies a tradition of debate about faith and assurance, a debate that was particularly acute at the time of the Reformation and immediately thereafter. Besides the

---

[1] Quoted by Avery Dulles, *The Assurance of Things Hoped For* (New York, 1994), 68.

words of Wesley's, it would be well to have before us some other representative statements of the relation between faith and assurance. The first example I shall take is from the Decrees of the Council of Trent:

> For even as no pious person ought to doubt of the mercy of God, of the merit of Christ, and of the virtue and efficacy of the sacraments, even so each one, when he regards himself, and his own weakness and indisposition, may have fear and apprehension touching his own grace; seeing that no one can know with a certainty of faith, which can not be subject to error, that he has obtained the grace of God.[2]

Note here the distinction between the objective and the subjective character of faith, faith and *the* faith; and that the certainty or assurance referred to is very strong—it 'can not be subject to error'. This looks very much like the territory of thin belief. And finally note that claims to have gained such inerrant assurance are absolutely forbidden. According to Trent, any claim to possess such infallible assurance of faith must be false, though presumably claims of a less well-grounded kind to possess assurance of faith are permitted; for example, the words of the Council seem to allow for the possession of a well-grounded though fallible assurance by a person that he or she has received the grace of God.

A second example may be taken from the Westminster Confession of Faith:

> This certainty is not a bare conjectural and probable persuasion, grounded upon a fallible hope; but an infallible assurance of faith, founded upon the divine truth of the promises of salvation, the inward evidence of those graces unto which these promises are made . . . This infallible assurance doth not so belong to the essence of faith, but that a true believer may wait long, and conflict with many difficulties, before he be partaker of it: yet, being enabled by the Spirit to know the things which are freely given him of God, he may, without extraordinary revelation, in the right use of ordinary means, attain thereunto.[3]

Note a similar strong conception of assurance as with the Council of Trent, 'infallible assurance', but note also that according to the Westminster divines a believer may have such infallible assurance, and indeed ought to have it.

---

[2] Session vi, ch. 9, 'Against the Vain Confidence of Heretics'; quoted in John Leith, *Creeds of the Churches* (New York, 1963), 413.

[3] Ch. 18, 'Of Assurance of Grace and Salvation', sects. ii–iii; quoted in Gerald Bray (ed.), *Documents of the English Reformation* (Cambridge, 1994), 500.

There seem to be two ways in which those who have discussed and emphasized the assurance of faith, as Wesley did, and as the Council of Trent and the Westminster Confession of Faith did, have taken it, and it may be helpful to highlight these for clarification. A distinction which runs fairly deeply through epistemology is that between knowledge by acquaintance and knowledge by description. Knowledge by description is knowledge that *p* in which *p* expresses a proposition, which is conveyed to the knower indirectly, say, by you telling me or by reading it. Knowledge by acquaintance is knowing that *p* in which *p* is conveyed to me directly, for example I know that the cat is on the mat because I see for myself that this is so.

Not surprisingly perhaps, since personal assurance is an epistemic concept, this distinction between the two kinds of knowledge applies to it also. I think the distinction can be illustrated from the historical examples of the treatment of assurance just given. In the case of Wesley, what he claims to have had is a direct assurance; what was 'given to him' was the direct awareness of the pardon of his sins, the direct conveying to his mind of the truth of a certain proposition, with the joy and sense of release that such an awareness brought. The truth that his sins were pardoned was directly conveyed to him. It is as if a person is told that someone else wishes to be his friend, believes this, and then suddenly and without warning experiences for himself the friendliness of that person.

In the cases of the Council of Trent and the Westminster Confession, the infallible personal assurance which the one denies and the other affirms to be possible looks much more like a case of knowledge by description, for the assurance which, according to the Confession, is founded upon the divine truth of the promises of salvation, together with the inward evidence of those graces unto which these promises are made, is an assurance that is gained through drawing inferences from the promises of God and one's own belief-state, inferences of the form 'God promises salvation to whoever believes; I believe; therefore I am saved.' Assurance in this sense comes as an inference, as the conclusion of a piece of syllogistic reasoning. It corresponds to knowledge by description.

In the next section I shall attempt to reconstruct the form of reasoning implicit in John Wesley's account of his conversion and to discuss aspects of its validity and invalidity; and in subsequent sections I shall discuss some of the relations between faith and conditionality. My purpose in this is to use some philosophy to highlight, and, I hope, cast some light upon, concrete issues to do with the nature of faith from the standpoint of the one who has faith, or suspects and hopes that he has it.

FAITH AND SELF-REFLECTION

Let us start by attempting to reconstruct Wesley's reasoning, looking first at a general point about the truth conditions of beliefs.

How are we to decide whether or not two beliefs are distinct? I shall claim that it is a sufficient condition for two beliefs being distinct that the propositions which are believed are distinct. (This may not be a necessary condition; whether it is so or not depends upon what the test of the distinctness of two propositions is.) Let us suppose that the proposition which forms one belief is that Jesus Christ came into the world to save sinners. That is a different belief from the belief that Muhammad Ali came into the world to save sinners; and a still different belief is that Jesus Christ came into the world to found the United Nations. If three people each believe one of these three propositions, then their beliefs are different because the objects of the beliefs, the propositions, are different; they each have a different meaning. I take it that this is fairly obvious.

Let us apply this distinction to Wesley's words: 'an assurance was given me that he had taken away *my* sins, even *mine*, and saved *me* from the law of sin and death.' The propositional object of Wesley's first belief is something like the following: 'that Jesus Christ came into the world to save from the law of sin and death'. But John Wesley's belief that Jesus Christ came into the world to save from the law of sin and death is a different belief from his belief that Jesus Christ came into the world to save himself, John Wesley, from the law of sin and death. Not only is it a different belief, but the proposition which forms the first belief does not entail the proposition that forms the second; one would need an additional proposition of the following kind: 'Jesus Christ has saved everyone without exception from the law of sin and death', which as a matter of fact John Wesley certainly did not believe. So perhaps that aspect of faith known as the assurance of faith is only of existential importance in religious communities which do not accept some form of universal salvation. The assurance of faith only matters if faith matters, and if it is true, or likely to be true, that not everyone has faith. If salvation is appropriated only by faith, and if not everyone has faith, then it is important to know whether or not one has it.

The propositional object of Wesley's second belief is 'that Jesus Christ came into the world to save me, John Wesley'. In order to be able to conclude that Jesus Christ came into the world to save him, John Wesley, from the belief that Jesus came into the world to save from the law of sin and death, John Wesley needs also to believe that he needs saving from the law of sin and death and, more crucially, he needs to believe that Jesus has saved him.

Let us set this out more formally. Consider the following argument:

(1) Wesley trusts Jesus Christ.
(2) Wesley believes that he trusts Jesus Christ.
(3) Anyone who trusts Jesus Christ is saved.
(4) Therefore, Wesley believes that he is saved.

This is an example of what is sometimes referred to as the principle of closure of belief under implication, and it is clearly an invalid form of argument. It does not follow that Wesley believes that he is saved, because although (3) is true (we are supposing), Wesley may not believe that (3) obtains in this particular case; indeed he may have no beliefs whatsoever about (3). So let us try the following argument:

(1*a*) Wesley believes that he trusts Jesus Christ.
(2*a*) Wesley believes that anyone who trusts Jesus Christ is saved.
(3*a*) Therefore, Wesley believes that he is saved.

This is better; this utilizes the much more plausible principle of closure of belief under believed implication. Can we therefore conclude that (3*a*) is true and that Wesley does believe that he is saved?

One condition for validly drawing this conclusion is not simply that (1*a*) and (2*a*) must each be believed by Wesley in order for (3*a*) to be true, but that each must be believed *together*. That is, in order for the conclusion (3*a*) to follow from the premises, it is necessary that the propositions expressed in (1*a*) and (2*a*) be fully integrated in Wesley's mind. Wesley himself needs to bring together his beliefs as expressed in (1*a*) and (2*a*), or they need to come together in some other way, and this argument offers no guarantee that this will happen. And we know from experience that this often does not happen. We may hold beliefs about many things and may fail to integrate them. One reason why we sometimes fail to integrate our beliefs is that we arrive at them at different times; another is that the emotional stake we have in one belief may be different from the stake that we have in another. Whatever the detailed explanation of such failures may be, the basic fact is that a person may have a belief without realizing its implications for another belief or beliefs that he holds.

There may be a variety of explanations as to why Wesley did not draw that conclusion, the conclusion that he believed that he was saved, until the time of his Aldersgate experience. It is as if, prior to the Aldersgate experience, he was not ready to believe (3*a*) on the basis of (1*a*) and (2*a*). Everything was ready for him to believe (3*a*), so to speak, but for some reason Wesley failed to register the connection between it and the other relevant beliefs that he held. Perhaps it was because until then he had been insufficiently reflective; or because until that moment (1*a*) was not true. Perhaps when (1*a*) became true, then, given the truth of (2*a*), the realization that (3*a*) is true immediately followed.

Perhaps we can distinguish between the following two sorts of case. The first sort of case is where Wesley does not realize that (3*a*) follows from (1*a*) and (2*a*), and therefore does not realize that the belief expressed in (3*a*) is open to him. We could express this rather graphically by saying that he may believe proposition (1*a*) with one part of his brain, and (2*a*) with another part. With one part of his brain he believes that he trusts Jesus Christ, while with another part of his brain he believes that anyone who trusts Jesus Christ is saved. These beliefs may be held apart for an indefinite period of time, but then they may come together all at once, as seems to have happened in Wesley's case. What the well-known words of Wesley appear to be describing are the cognitive and other effects of integrating these various beliefs or, more exactly, of these beliefs coming to be integrated. This integration enabled John Wesley to affirm that he believed that Jesus Christ had saved *him*, to express his assurance in the well-known words, and to benefit from the joy and peace that this belief warranted.

A second sort of case is where Wesley recognizes the connection between (1*a*) and (2*a*) but is disposed not to believe that he is saved because he cannot bring himself to draw that momentous inference, as a person may not be able to believe that he has won the National Lottery even though it is true that he has, and that he has good evidence that he has. What exactly these factors so disposing him were or may have been in Wesley's case is, from a strictly philosophical standpoint, an irrelevance. All that we need to recognize is that the premises may be held by the same person at the same time, but may also for various reasons be held apart.

It may be said that the above explanation is not to the point because Wesley's words are better interpreted as a case of knowledge by acquaintance rather than knowledge by description. But I think the same problems and their solution may apply in the case of knowledge by acquaintance. Thus:

(1) Wesley believes that his heart is strangely warmed.
(2) The strange warming of Wesley's heart is the granting of assurance that his sins were taken away.
(3) Therefore, Wesley believed that his sins were taken away.

The same invalidity is apparent; and the same solution, or possible solution, is at hand, namely,

(1) Wesley believes that his heart is strangely warmed.
(2a) Wesley believes that the strange warming of his heart is the granting of assurance that his sins were taken away.
(3) Therefore, Wesley believed that his sins were taken away.

But here, as before, this is a solution only on the assumption that Wesley has fully integrated beliefs on the matter, that the beliefs expressed in (1) and (2a) are held together by him.

So the possession of faith, and self-reflection about such a possession, involve two distinct beliefs, for each belief has a different propositional object. To believe in Jesus Christ, to have in faith in him, is a distinct belief from the belief that you, the believer, believe in Jesus Christ. Because they are two distinct beliefs they cannot be the same belief. Not only are they distinct beliefs, one belief is about another belief of the same person. These beliefs can be held by the same person at the same time, but for various reasons they may be held apart; when they are held together they are sufficient, other things being equal, to ensure the assurance of faith.

While we are on the subject of the consequences for faith and assurance of some aspects of the logic of belief, consider the following argument:

(1) Wesley trusts in Jesus Christ.
(2) Wesley knows that whoever trusts in Christ is saved.
(3) Therefore Wesley is warranted in concluding that he is saved.

This, I suggest, is an invalid argument, at least if it is assumed that trust involves belief. What more is required to render it valid? What we need is an additional premise about the nature of belief, or about the nature of trust in so far as it involves belief, a principle such as

If *A* believes that *p* then he knows that he believes that *p*.

But this is an implausible principle, given that belief is often highly dispositional in character and that a person's beliefs may also be accompanied by self-forgetfulness. However, it may be argued that this additional principle is unnecessary if it is necessarily the case that any instance of doxastic trust involves self-aware belief. But this seems doubtful, for the principle

If *A* trusts *B* then he knows that he trusts *B*

is equally doubtful.

The first-person form of this argument does not appear to be similarly defective. That is, the following argument,

(1) I trust in Jesus Christ;
(2) I know that whoever trusts in Christ is saved;
(3) Therefore I am warranted in concluding that I am saved,

appears to be sound, because it is plausible to suppose that whoever (1) is true of also knows that (1) is true of him. But even this may be disputed because it may be that a person can both trust Christ and know that he does, while doing so in a self-forgetful and unselfconscious manner. The trust and the knowledge of the trust may fail to be integrated. If so, then the above argument may still be invalid. But perhaps one could amend the argument as follows:

(1*a*) I know that I trust Christ.
(2) I know that whoever trusts Christ is saved.
(3) Therefore I am warranted in concluding that I am saved.

And this argument appears to be valid.

It may be objected that the very idea of self-reflection of this sort is theoretically defective because it involves an infinite regress. If it is possible to raise the question of whether I believe that I believe, is it not also possible to raise the question of whether I believe that I believe that I believe? I think that it is theoretically possible to do this, but it is not clear why this makes the very idea of self-reflection incoherent. For though it is theoretically possible to do this, it rapidly becomes impossible to distinguish one step in the regress from the others, and the interest in or informativeness of doing so rapidly diminishes.

But let us suppose that self-reflection takes place in order to ascertain whether the belief that I think I hold I do in fact hold. Does not the fact that it is possible to iterate beliefs-that in this way become equivalent to some form of scepticism? Not necessarily. Whether or not it does so depends upon what is to count as the standard of evidence for the belief.[4]

So this is the first principle about belief which I wish to note, that beliefs are distinguished by the propositions believed; and hence that the belief that *p*, and the belief that I believe that *p*, are distinct beliefs; and hence that on most accounts of faith, and certainly on Wesley's, faith must be distinguished from the assurance of faith.

FAITH AND CONDITIONALITY

I have so far tried to offer a clarification of the language of the personal assurance of faith such as one finds in John Wesley and in many other Christian writers.

From the previous discussion of Wesley's Aldersgate experience it is clear that it is possible to talk about faith and its conditions, conditions of the truth of the belief component of faith, and those epistemic conditions which make it evident to a believer that he is indeed a believer, and so may come to personal assurance of the fact. Faith, if it has a belief component, has truth conditions, the conditions for the truth of the proposition that is believed. And similarly for the second-order belief, the belief that one believes.

But there is a type of religious or theological thinking which shuns all such talk of faith and assurance, because in its view such talk is based upon a fundamental misapprehension about religious faith. On this view faith is by definition unconditional and to suppose that there is a viable distinction, such as Wesley supposed, between faith and the assurance of faith is to miss the central point about faith's

---

[4] D. H. Mellor has argued that consciousness is to be understood in terms of believing that one believes (or doubts, or hopes, or . . .): 'Conscious Belief', *Proceedings of the Aristotelian Society*, 78 (1977/8), 87–101. See also his 'Consciousness and Degrees of Belief', in D. H. Mellor (ed.), *Prospects for Pragmatism* (Cambridge, 1980).

unconditionality. The reason for thinking that faith is unconditional is because it is claimed that if the grace of God itself is unconditional then neither faith nor anything else can be a condition of receiving or enjoying that grace. Otherwise the unconditional character of divine grace would be subverted. If grace is unconditional and faith conveys or apprehends this grace, then faith must also be unconditional; this seems to be the argument.

It is not appropriate for me here to comment on the theological grounds that lie behind the claimed unconditionality of faith. What is of philosophical interest here are remarks about the very idea of the conditionality of faith. In the remainder of this chapter I propose to try, as far as possible, to abstract from the theological justification of any such position and to look at two arguments for the unconditionality of faith, and therefore for the irrelevance of assurance, which seem to me to rest on questionable claims or assumptions about the nature of conditions. I shall call these claims the *faith and conditions argument* and the *grounds substitution argument*. Let us look at each of them in turn.

THE FAITH AND CONDITIONS ARGUMENT

I shall endeavour to set out this argument in the words of Karl Barth. This is what Barth says in his *Church Dogmatics*, in a commentary on the same passage from the Council of Trent that I quoted from earlier:

> Could he [Paul] have forbidden it to a Christian as a *vana et omni pietati remota fiducia*, the very words of the Tridentium (c.9), to cling in faith and to find comfort in the fact that his sins are forgiven? Could he have regarded it as a 'heretical and schismatic' opinion that Christian faith has an unconditional and not a conditional assurance of this, and that so far as it does not have this unconditional assurance it is not the true Christian faith which justifies a man? Where did he ever say, and how could he possibly have said, that (c.9) although the Christian ought not to doubt the mercy of God, the merit of Christ and the power of the sacraments, yet in view of his own *infirmitas* and *indispositio* even in faith there can be no absolute assurance *de sua gratia*, in the question of whether there is grace for him?[5]

---

[5] Karl Barth, *Church Dogmatics. Volume IV: The Doctrine of Reconciliation*, pt. 1, trans. G. W. Bromiley (Edinburgh, 1956), 625.

We may take Barth's remarks here as representative of the sort of view that (as we have noted) a number of theologians and religious thinkers would accept, namely that all grace, including the grace by which a person is assured of the forgiveness of sins, is unconditional grace. In what follows we shall assume that this view of divine grace is true; grace is unconditional. However, it is held to be a consequence of this view that to raise the question of whether one has faith is to make a logical and also perhaps a theological mistake rather than to make a legitimate religious enquiry. For to raise the question of the assurance of faith is, in Barth's view, to call in question the very unconditionality of grace.

In the first half of the chapter we have seen reason to doubt the logical coherence of the position that Barth expresses here. For if Christian faith gives unconditional assurance in the way Barth expresses it, then it must have a transparent reflexivity to it such that if *A* has faith in Christ then necessarily *A* knows that he has faith in Christ. If Barth is correct then it must be *part of what it means* to have faith in Christ that one knows that one does. Christian assurance is incorrigible in the sense that if a person truly believes in Christ then he knows for sure that he does; he cannot be mistaken. So no one can have faith in Christ, and at the same time wonder whether or not he does so and then later discover that he does.

There is of course nothing to stop Barth or anyone else defining (or redefining) faith and assurance in this way. But if one does so then these terms lose some of their important connections of meaning with faith and assurance as they are used in contexts other than Christian theology, or in the Christian religion. For as used in non-theological contexts assurance does not have the transparent reflexivity or incorrigibility that Barth here claims for it. And there are good reasons for this. For as we have argued earlier in this chapter, and throughout the book, faith involves belief, and belief can be present in highly dispositional or intuitive forms. And faith also involves trust, which may be similarly dispositional and be present while at the same time remaining unnoticed. A person may have such dispositions—beliefs and trust—and be unaware of them, or even deny that he has them; we have many beliefs of which we are unaware, and trust people and things without being aware that we do. If Barth is correct that faith in Christ is sufficient for the forgiveness of sins, and I have faith in Christ, then on Barth's understanding it follows *ex vi termini* that, since I know that I believe, then I am assured of forgiveness. We have already seen reason to doubt the cogency of this position, and I shall not repeat the argument here.

What is of more interest at this point is not Barth's remarks about assurance, but his remarks about faith, which are logically prior to the point about assurance. For Barth the only kind of genuine faith is unconditional faith. The point of making this claim, I take it, is that conditional faith is faith that is impure or compromised in character, since it does not reflect the truly gracious basis of faith, and so is not true faith.

What Barth appears to be saying is that granted that belief is a propositional attitude, the only appropriate propositions for the assurance of faith are propositions which are unconditionally true, the truth of which is not conditioned upon any state of the believer. In particular, assurance is belief which does not depend on the believer believing some proposition or other. It is assurance without belief. So unconditional assurance is assurance that is not dependent upon or in any way supervenes upon a belief, much less assurance which depends for its validity on whether or not I believe that I have faith. What might examples of such unconditional faith be? One might call to mind at this point the notorious remark of Paul Tillich: 'Do not seek for anything; do not perform anything; do not intend anything. *Simply accept the fact that you are accepted!*'

Let us suppose that a rough synonym for the first occurrence of 'accept' in this sentence is 'believe'; then what Tillich is saying seems to be a clear case of unconditional acceptance or belief. Someone who accepts that he is accepted, just like that, does so unconditionally. (Of course, if he does so because Tillich tells him to, then that is another matter, for then he accepts that he is accepted because he believes someone else, and the conditionality of faith reappears.) The crucial thing, from a logical point of view, is that if a person is accepted, whatever precisely being accepted may mean, then his acceptance, being past- or perfectly tensed, is over and done with. And if it is over and done with then nothing in the present, such as whether or not he believes some particular proposition or other, can affect the truth of this past-tensed or perfectly tensed state of affairs.

If faith is accepting that I am accepted, then the fact that I failed to obey Tillich's injunction and failed to accept that I am accepted would not affect the fact of my acceptance, because my acceptance, being in the past, is completed, and cannot now be the subject of any further conditions. For on the Tillichian view, the fact is that I am accepted, and nothing now or ever can influence this fact one way or another; certainly no state of mine, such as belief or acceptance or doubt, can have any influence upon this fact. It is not a condition of being accepted that I accept the truth of some proposition, not even the proposition that I am accepted; the most that can be hoped for from me and expected of me, according to Tillich, is that I may come to recognize that I am accepted, that I accept it. Such acceptance may lead to the elimination of religious anxiety, and perhaps anxiety of other kinds, but it won't influence or affect the basic fact of the matter, which was, and is, that I am accepted.

What has happened here, it seems, is not so much that faith and the assurance of faith have become conflated in a way that (as we noticed in our earlier discussion) embodies a logical confusion, but that faith has taken on certain of the features of assurance. Just as the absence of assurance may not affect the reality of faith, so, in the view of Barth and Tillich, the absence of faith does not affect the reality of one's acceptance. Faith may exist without assurance, just as acceptance may exist in ignorance of the fact. To suppose that assurance might be the assurance of faith (in the way in which, say, Wesley understood it) would be to conditionalize divine grace, to interpose something between the believer and his acceptance, namely the presence and exercise of faith.

I hope that this is a reasonable reading of what theologians such as Barth and Tillich may have meant by the unconditionality of faith. As I have said, it is not my place here to say whether Barth and Tillich do or do not have good theological reasons for the positions that they take on the unconditionality of faith, understood in this way.

What I wish to try to show now is that while this view of faith may be sufficient for ensuring its unconditionality, it is not necessary. That is, the Wesley position, as I shall call it, the position that makes a distinction between faith and its assurance, does not entail that faith is conditional in any sense which subverts the unconditionality of divine grace; and if what is of concern to Barth and Tillich, in elaborating their views of faith and acceptance, is to preserve the unconditionality of divine grace, they will have nothing to fear from the Wesley position.

Suppose that it is true that

Christ has accepted me whatever now happens;

then I shall be saved no matter whether I have faith in Christ or not. This is certainly unconditional salvation. But suppose the Wesley position is true; suppose that it is true that

Christ will save me only if I trust him.

My enjoyment of salvation would then certainly be conditioned upon faith. But it would be a travesty to suppose that this conditional proposition, the proposition that Christ will save me only if I trust him, was the *object* of my trust, and that as a consequence my *trust* has a conditional character. No, the trust called for in this proposition, as its wording makes plain, is trust in Christ. This proposition is thus a second-order proposition, a proposition which is, in effect, a comment on the nature of the trust which a person enjoys if he trusts Christ.

Faith may be wholly and unreservedly in Christ; Christ alone, with no conditions attached, may be the object of faith. But suppose that (unlike Barth and Tillich, perhaps) a person's theology (like Wesley's, perhaps) is such that only if a person has faith in Christ will he be saved. It would be a travesty to suppose that the object of Wesley's trust then became that conditional proposition, and that as a consequence such a person was imposing conditions in the place of Christ, and so compromising the unconditionality of divine grace.

We can develop this final point by considering the second argument about the conditionality of faith, which I have called the grounds substitution argument.

THE GROUNDS SUBSTITUTION ARGUMENT

This argument may also be introduced by a quotation from Karl Barth:

Christian faith has an unconditional and not a conditional assurance of this (viz. the forgiveness of sins), and that so far as it does not have this unconditional assurance it is not the true Christian faith which justifies a man.[6]

Once again, two things need separating here: the conditions that have to be true for faith to be genuine faith; and the conditions that have to be true for a person to know that his faith is genuine. We

[6] Barth, *Church Dogmatics*, iv. 1, 625.

need to observe carefully the distinction between faith and the assurance of faith that we discussed earlier. According to Barth, one thing
that faith needs in order to be genuine is to have the appropriate
object of trust, Christ. Any state that has an inappropriate object of
trust is not true faith. This much may be agreed.

But Barth appears to believe that any attempt that a person may
make to know that his faith is genuine is to substitute an inappropriate object of trust for the appropriate object of trust, Christ. But it is
hard to see how an enquiry into whether one's faith is genuine is a
case of relying on or trusting in one's own activity and accomplish-
ment instead of trusting in Christ. It is hard to see how fulfilling the
latter conditions, which are (I argued earlier) different from fulfilling
the former, means that gaining the evidence of the genuineness of the
faith which relies upon Christ unconditionally (i.e. upon Christ
alone) conditionalizes and so invalidates the unconditionality of
faith. Faith, and the object of faith, is one thing; evidence of the possession of faith is another.

So a second understanding of the phrase 'conditional faith' is that
faith is conditional if it is appropriate to seek, or necessary to seek,
evidence of its genuineness in the one who purportedly has it. Then
awareness of the genuineness of the faith, or of the fact that it is not
genuine, would be conditioned upon whether or not it gives evidence
of itself. But this fact about how one comes to learn certain truths
about oneself, how one comes to learn whether or not one is truly a
believer, does not subvert the unconditional or unreserved character
of the trust; it would only do so if the evidence that a person has that
he trusts Christ is the same as the grounds he has for trusting Christ.
But to suppose that this evidence is the same, or could be the same,
would be to make a serious confusion. I may be a UK citizen unconditionally, by birth, but I may not know this. Suppose that I then
take steps to investigate the question and discover that I am indeed a
citizen by birth. Does the evidence that I now possess for this fact
subvert the unconditionality of the fact itself?

For salvation to be unconditional and therefore truly gracious it
cannot be conditioned on any state of the recipient; this much may
be granted. But as it stands the expression 'salvation is unconditional' is ambiguous. It may mean: the *fact* of salvation cannot be
conditioned on any human state; or it may mean: the *application* or
personal enjoyment of salvation cannot be conditioned on any human
state. Understood in the first way the expression may be true, but

understood in the second way it is false. To assume that these ways of understanding the expression mean the same thing is to show an insufficient appreciation of the diverse ways in which conditions may be invoked.

One might at this point simply stipulate that faith which is not utterly self-forgetful is not true faith; that as soon as elements of doubt, or of self-reflection, arise, then faith is necessarily corrupted. It is certainly possible to take such a view; but as with any stipulation, there is no intellectual compulsion to accept it.

BIBLIOGRAPHY

ALSTON, WILLIAM P., *Perceiving God* (Ithaca, NY, 1991).
—— 'Swinburne on Faith and Belief', in Alan G. Padgett (ed.), *Reason and the Christian Religion* (Oxford, 1994).
AQUINAS, THOMAS, *Summa contra Gentiles*, i, trans. A. C. Pegis (Garden City, NY, 1955).
—— *Summa Theologiae, Part 1, Questions 1–13*, ed. Thomas Gilby (Garden City, NY, 1969).
AUDI, ROBERT, 'Faith, Belief and Rationality', in James E. Tomberlin (ed.), *Philosophical Perspectives 5: Philosophy of Religion, 1991* (Atascadero, Calif., 1991).
BARTH, KARL, *Church Dogmatics. Volume IV: The Doctrine of Reconciliation*, pt. 1, trans. G. W. Bromiley (Edinburgh, 1956).
BONJOUR, LAURENCE, *The Structure of Empirical Knowledge* (Cambridge, Mass., 1985).
BOUWSMA, O. K., 'Faith, Evidence and Proof', in J. L. Craft and R. Hustwit (ed.), *Without Proof or Evidence: Essays of O. K. Bouwsma* (Lincoln, Nebr., 1984).
BRÜMMER, VINCENT, *Speaking of a Personal God* (Cambridge, 1992).
—— *What are we Doing when we Pray?* (London, 1984).
BULTMANN, RUDOLF, 'Bultmann Replies to his Critics', in *Kerygma and Myth*, i (London, 1972).
BURNYEAT, MYLES, 'The Sceptic in his Place and Time', in Richard Rorty, J. B. Schneewind, and Quentin Skinner (eds.), *Philosophy in History* (Cambridge, 1984).
BUTLER, JOSEPH, *The Analogy of Religion*, in *Works*, ed. W. E. Gladstone (Oxford, 1897), vol. i.
CALVIN, JOHN, *Institutes of the Christian Religion*, trans. F. L. Battles (London, 1960).
DE SOUSA, RONALD, *The Rationality of Emotion* (Cambridge, Mass., 1987).
DULLES, AVERY, *The Assurance of Things Hoped For* (New York, 1994).
EVANS, DONALD M., *The Logic of Self-involvement* (London, 1963).
GEACH, P. T., 'Assertion', in *Logic Matters* (Oxford, 1972).
GUNTON, COLIN E., *The One, the Three and the Many* (Cambridge, 1993).
HARRISON, BERNARD, 'Moral Judgment, Action and Emotion', *Philosophy*, 59 (1984), 295–322.
HELM, PAUL, *Belief Policies* (Cambridge, 1994).
—— *Faith and Understanding* (Edinburgh, 1997).

HELM, PAUL, 'John Calvin, the *Sensus Divinitatis*, and the Noetic Effects of Sin', *International Journal for the Philosophy of Religion*, 43 (1998), 87–107.

—— 'The Perfect and the Particular', Inaugural Lecture, King's College, London, 1994.

—— 'Prayer and Providence', in Gijsbert van den Brink, Luco J. van den Brom, and Marcel Sarot (eds.), *Christian Faith and Philosophical Theology* (Kampen, 1992).

JAMES, WILLIAM, *The Will to Believe and Other Essays* (New York, 1917).

KENNY, ANTHONY, *What is Faith?* (Oxford, 1992).

KIERKEGAARD, SØREN, *Concluding Unscientific Postscript to 'Philosophical Fragments'*, ed. and trans. H. V. Hong and E. H. Hong (Princeton, NJ, 1992).

KRETZMANN, NORMAN, 'Evidence against Anti-evidentialism', in Kelly James Clark (ed.), *Our Knowledge of God: Essays on Natural and Philosophical Theology* (Dordrecht, 1992).

LEITH, JOHN, *Creeds of the Churches* (New York, 1963).

LOCKE, JOHN, *An Essay Concerning Human Understanding*, ed. J. W. Yolton (London, 1961).

MELLOR, D. H., 'Conscious Belief', *Proceedings of the Aristotelian Society*, 78 (1977/8), 87–101.

—— 'Consciousness and Degrees of Belief', in D. H. Mellor (ed.), *Prospects for Pragmatism* (Cambridge, 1980).

MITCHELL, BASIL, *Faith and Criticism* (Oxford, 1994).

—— *The Justification of Religious Belief* (London, 1973).

NUSSBAUM, MARTHA, *Poetic Justice* (Boston, 1995).

PHILLIPS, D. Z., *Faith and Philosophical Enquiry* (London, 1970).

PLANTINGA, ALVIN, 'Reason and Belief in God', in Alvin Plantinga and Nicholas Wolterstorff (eds.), *Faith and Rationality* (Notre Dame, Ind., 1983).

ROBERTS, ROBERT C., 'Emotions as Access to Religious Truths', *Faith and Philosophy*, 9 (1992), 83–94.

ROSS, JAMES, 'Cognitive Finality', in Linda Zagzebski (ed.), *Rational Faith* (Notre Dame, Ind., 1993).

SCHLESINGER, GEORGE, *New Perspectives on Old-time Religion* (Oxford, 1988).

SESSIONS, WILLIAM LAD, *The Concept of Faith* (Ithaca, NY, 1994).

SWINBURNE, RICHARD, *The Christian God*, (Oxford, 1994).

—— *The Coherence of Theism* (Oxford, 1977).

—— *The Existence of God* (Oxford, 1979).

—— *Faith and Reason* (Oxford, 1981).

—— *Revelation: From Metaphor to Analogy* (Oxford, 1994).

TANNER, KATHRYN, 'Jesus Christ', in Colin E. Gunton (ed.), *The Cambridge Companion to Christian Doctrine* (Cambridge, 1997).

VAN INWAGEN, PETER, 'It is Wrong, Everywhere, Always, and for Anyone, to Believe Anything upon Insufficient Evidence', in Daniel Howard-Snyder and Jeff Jordan (eds.), *Faith, Freedom and Rationality* (London, 1996).

'The Westminster Confession of Faith' (1647), in Gerald Bray (ed.), *Documents of the English Reformation* (Cambridge, 1994).

WESTPHAL, MEROLD, 'Taking St. Paul Seriously: Sin as an Epistemological Category', in Thomas P. Flint (ed.), *Christian Philosophy* (Notre Dame, Ind., 1990).

INDEX

acceptance 173
Alston, W. 36
Anselm 7
antinomianism 100
Apostles' Creed 50
Aquinas, T. 18–19, 24–5, 45, 142
assurance
  and inference 163
  infallible 164
  unconditional 172–3
Audi, R. 4, 22

Barth, K. 13, 43, 120, 171-6
beatific vision 143
belief
  basic 31, 37n.
  degrees of, 19
  and faith, 20
  thin and thick 105n., 160n.
  and will 146–7
beliefs 165
believing and understanding 8–9
bias 89
BonJour, L. 47
Bouwsma, O.K. 132n.
Brümmer, V. 129
Brunner, E. 13, 120
Buber, M. 120
Bultmann, R. 114–15, 118
Burnyeat, M. 103, 108

Calvin, J. 84n., 88, 89n., 91
Christian faith 45, 50, 54, 60
Christian theism 39
Christianity 2, 47, 54, 119
circularity 58–9, 100
coherence 48, 53n.
coherentism 44n., 48–9, 71
conditional faith 175–6
Council of Trent 163n., 171
covenant 106, 117, 123
cumulative case 77

danger 79
deism 123
deists 76, 118

Descartes, R. 26, 33–4, 76, 103
De Sousa, R. 97
determinism 131
dispositions 88, 157
distrust 109
divine simplicity 93

Enlightenment 103
entrusting 125, 151
epistemic justification 22
Evans, D. 59
evidence 72–3, 91
  and grounds 28
  standards of 170
  subjective 159–60, 162
evidential deficiency 20
evidential proportion 20
evidentialism 80, 90, 98–9
experience 5, 74

faith 107
  and acceptance 173
  and assurance 159n.
  and awareness 172
  and belief 141n.
  as certain 19, 37
  and conditions 170n. 175–6
  as doxastic 4–5, 15–16
  as evidential 16–7, 115
  as fiducial 19, 37, 115
  and good will 153
  and justification, 140
  Lutheran view 115, 140n.
  merit of 116
  Pragmatist view 115, 140n.
  as non-propositional 14
  and risk 156–7
  Thomist view 115, 140n.
  and virtue 138n.
  as voluntary 152
  and works 139, 157
Farmer, H.H. 120
foundationalism 22n., 38n., 52
Frege, G. 11
fundamental beliefs 31n.
fundamental propositions 30

God
  concept of 46
  existence of 7–8, 34, 81
  moral character of 93 n.
  nature of 94–5
  of the philosophers 104–5, 106
  promises of 18
  trust in 109–10
guilt 81

Harrison, B. 127 n. 130
Heim, K. 120
Hobbes, T. 89
hope 116, 148
Hume, D. 56, 93, 94, 120, 145, 155

incorrigibility 154
indeterminism 129, 131, 135
indifference 105
individualism 120
ineffability 60, 74
insulation 103
integration of beliefs 167
integrity, 125
interests 125 n.
introspection 160
intuition 70
'I—thou' relations 121

James, W. 92, 99, 107
James Principle, The 14, 41, 58, 59, 102
judgement 69 n.

Kant, I. 76, 80, 112 n.
Kenny, A. 9, 20, 21, 27 n., 42 n., 62, 65
Kierkegaard, S. 6, 104, 118, 149
knowledge 7, 156, 164, 168
Kuhn, T. 68–9

Lamont, D. 120
linear reasoning 39 n., 43 n.
Locke, J. 3, 26, 76, 82, 87, 90
Luther, M. 75, 81, 114, 142–3

Macmurray, J. 120
Marx, K. 75
materialism 97 n.
memory 54, 61, 72
merit 146 n., 151-2
  Roman Catholic view of, 116
Mitchell, B.G. 63 n., 66 n., 87
Moore, G.E. 149
moral block 91

moral facts 101
moral nature 91, 92, 96–7, 100

natural theology 23 n., 39 n., 42, 46–7,
  51, 105 107
Niebuhr, R. 120
noetic structure 26, 33, 84

objectivity 77, 99
  denial of 12
Oman, J. 159

Paley, W. 104
parity of faiths 62
Pascal, B. 92, 147
Pascal's Wager 82, 147
person-relative beliefs 30, 67, 71, 72 n.,
  74 n., 87
Phillips, D.Z. 7 n. 63
philosophy of religion 1-3
pietism 159
Plantinga, A. 21, 24 n., 41, 43, 78–9,
  84–5
practical reason 112 n.
problem of evil 97
projection 89
proof 77
propositional attitudes 124
propositional objects 165
providence 57
Puritanism 159

rationality 22–3, 38, 80, 110, 148
reasonableness 12–13
Reformation 52, 106, 139
Reformed epistemology 78 n., 84
regress, infinite 70, 169–70
Reid T. 130
relativism 12
religion 2, 10
  nature of 78 n.
  rationality of 66–7
revelation 40 n., 141
risk 156
Ross, J. 104

Schesinger, G. 2
self 30
self-evidence 30, 35
sensus divinitatis 86
strong foundationalism 25 n .
subjectivism 12, 77
subjects 120–1

summum bonum 131
suppression 89
Swinburne, R. 87, 115 n., 130, 139 n.
 on faith 19–20
 on revelation, 40
 on coherence 49

Tanner, K. 9
Temple, W. 120
tenacity 105, 150, 155
Tertullian 18
testimony 19
theology 96
 metaphysical 113
thick belief
 instability of 112
this-ness 136
Tillich, P. 173–5
trust 17, 20, 105 n., 110 n., 160–1
 and belief 145 n.
 and certainty 143
 degrees of 156
 and desire 124
 and evidence 132 n.

and freedom 129
and good 17
mutuality of 126
phenomenology of 121
as unconditional 64, 128
trusting 121 n. 150

unbelief 87 n.
understanding 8 n.
universal salvation 165

visions 76, 161

wants 87, 88
Ward, K. 13
web of belief 43 n., 52
 personal 31–2
Wesley, J. 162 n., 174
Westminster Confession of Faith,
 163–4
wishing 99
Wittgenstein, L. 31–3, 113
world view 96